INDIAN GALLERY

Mary Sayre Haverstock

INDIAN GALLERY

The Story of
George Catlin

Four Winds Press ❦ *New York*

DISCARDED

Published by Four Winds Press
A division of Scholastic Magazines, Inc., New York, N.Y.

Copyright © 1973 by Mary Sayre Haverstock

Printed in the United States of America
Library of Congress Catalogue Card Number: 72-87075

To John Reece
A Good Companion
1956 §§ 1971

Author's Note

George Catlin was one of the best story-tellers of his day. Many times in this book, I have quoted conversations and incidents as Catlin himself reported them, for I could think of no way to improve upon the artist's own vivid language. Many of these passages first appeared in Catlin's 1841 *Letters and Notes,* (see bibliography). In addition, I was particularly fortunate to have the kind permission of Marjorie Catlin Roehm to quote from the personal letters of the Catlin family, now on deposit at the Bancroft Library of the University of California, at Berkeley.

For their invaluable help in locating and interpreting Catlin's less familiar paintings, I am deeply indebted to William H. Truettner, Associate Curator of Eighteenth and Nineteenth Century Painting and Sculpture, National Collection of Fine Arts, and William P. Campbell, Assistant Curator, National Gallery of Art. And though hard pressed by his own busy schedule, John C. Ewers, Senior Ethnologist, Smithsonian Institution, was kind enough to point out some of the manuscript's more glaring faults, in time for me to correct them. For this I am most grateful of all.

Mary Sayre Haverstock

Contents

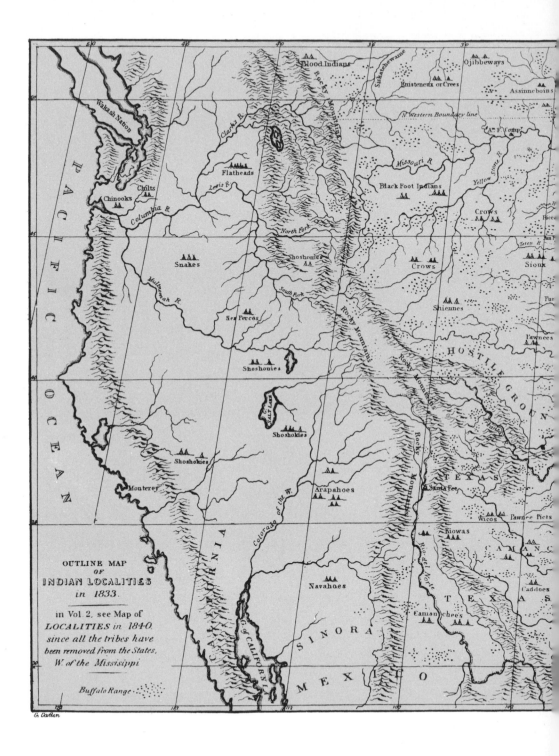

OUTLINE MAP
OF
INDIAN LOCALITIES
in 1833.

in Vol. 2, see Map of
LOCALITIES in 1840.
since all the tribes have
been removed from the States,
W. of the Missisippi

Buffalo Range

G. Catlin

PACIFIC OCEAN

Wakash Nation

Chilts

Chinooks

Columbia R.

Clarks R.

Lewis R.

Flatheads

North Fork

Snakes

Multnomah R.

Nez Percos

South Fork

Shoshonies

Shoshonies

G.t SALT LAKE

Shoshokies

Shoshokies

Monterey

Colorado of the W.

CALIFORNIA

Arapahoes

Navahoes

G.f CALIFORNIA

SINORA

MEXICO

Blood Indians

Rocky Mountains

Siskatchewawine

Bristeneux or Crees

Ojibbeways

Assinneboins

N Western Boundary line

A. F. Comp.

Missouri R.

Black Foot Indians

Yellow Stone R.

Crows

Faces

Shoshonies

Crows

Sioux

Teton R.

Shiennes

Fur

Pawnees

HOSTILE GROUN

Rocky Mountains

Rocky Mountains

Santa Fee

TEXAS

Kiowas

Wicos

Pawnee Picts

CAMANC

Rio del Norte

Caddoes

Camanchees

TEXAS

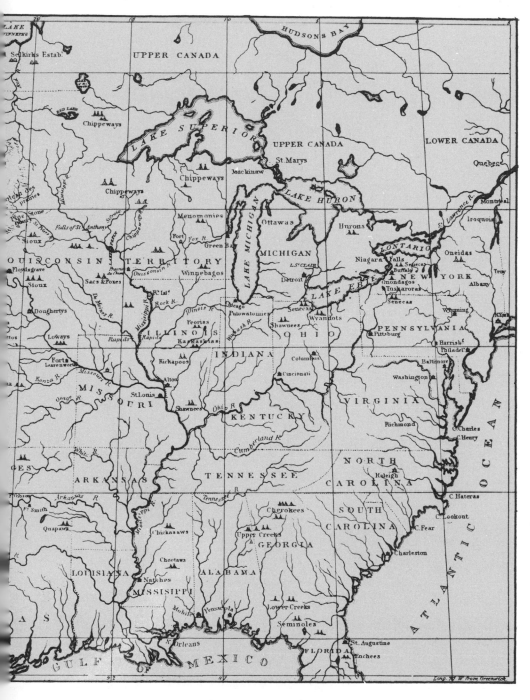

🖐 *This is Catlin's own map published in 1841 in his book* LETTERS AND NOTES ON THE MANNERS, CUSTOMS, AND CONDITIONS OF THE NORTH AMERICAN INDIANS, *showing the location of various tribes he had visited and painted.*

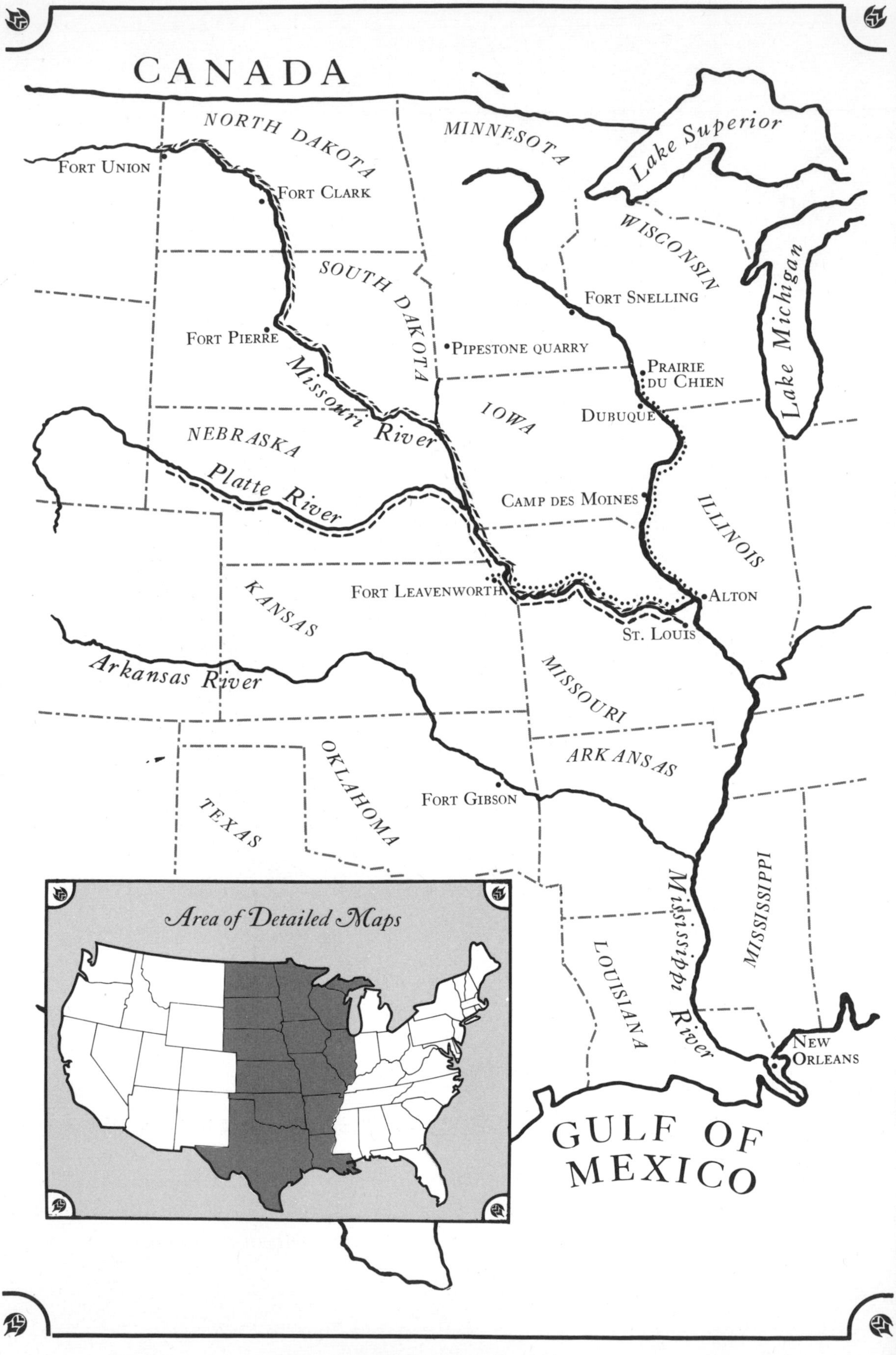

CANADA

NORTH DAKOTA

FORT UNION

• FORT CLARK

SOUTH DAKOTA

MINNESOTA

Lake Superior

WISCONSIN

FORT PIERRE

Missouri River

NEBRASKA

Platte River

KANSAS

Arkansas River

FORT LEAVENWORTH

• PIPESTONE QUARRY

IOWA

• FORT SNELLING

PRAIRIE DU CHIEN

DUBUQUE

Lake Michigan

CAMP DES MOINES

ILLINOIS

• ALTON

ST. LOUIS

MISSOURI

ARKANSAS

FORT GIBSON

OKLAHOMA

TEXAS

LOUISIANA

Mississippi River

MISSISSIPPI

NEW ORLEANS

GULF OF MEXICO

Area of Detailed Maps

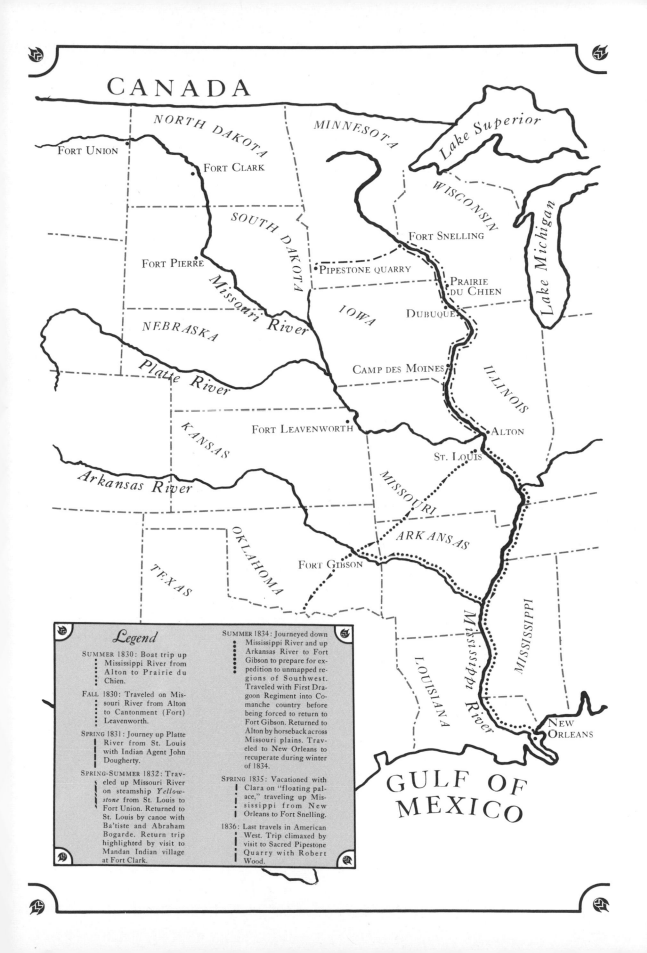

CANADA

NORTH DAKOTA

FORT UNION

FORT CLARK

MINNESOTA

Lake Superior

SOUTH DAKOTA

WISCONSIN

FORT PIERRE

FORT SNELLING

Lake Michigan

Missouri River

PIPESTONE QUARRY

PRAIRIE DU CHIEN

NEBRASKA

IOWA

DUBUQUE

Platte River

CAMP DES MOINES

ILLINOIS

KANSAS

FORT LEAVENWORTH

ALTON

Arkansas River

ST. LOUIS

MISSOURI

OKLAHOMA

ARKANSAS

TEXAS

FORT GIBSON

Mississippi River

MISSISSIPPI

LOUISIANA

NEW ORLEANS

GULF OF MEXICO

Legend

SUMMER 1830: Boat trip up Mississippi River from Alton to Prairie du Chien.

FALL 1830: Traveled on Missouri River from Alton to Cantonment (Fort) Leavenworth.

SPRING 1831: Journey up Platte River from St. Louis with Indian Agent John Dougherty.

SPRING-SUMMER 1832: Traveled up Missouri River on steamship *Yellowstone* from St. Louis to Fort Union. Returned to St. Louis by canoe with Ba'tiste and Abraham Bogarde. Return trip highlighted by visit to Mandan Indian village at Fort Clark.

SUMMER 1834: Journeyed down Mississippi River and up Arkansas River to Fort Gibson to prepare for expedition to unmapped regions of Southwest. Traveled with First Dragoon Regiment into Comanche country before being forced to return to Fort Gibson. Returned to Alton by horseback across Missouri plains. Traveled to New Orleans to recuperate during winter of 1834.

SPRING 1835: Vacationed with Clara on "floating palace," traveling up Mississippi from New Orleans to Fort Snelling.

1836: Last travels in American West. Trip climaxed by visit to Sacred Pipestone Quarry with Robert Wood.

INDIAN GALLERY

Preface

WHEREVER HE WENT, GEORGE CATLIN tacked a sign to his door. The sign said simply, *"G. Catlin, Artist."*

No advertisement ever revealed so little when it might have said so much. It might have said: "G. Catlin, Artist, Traveler, Anthropologist, Writer, Lecturer, Lawyer, Buffalo Hunter, Gold Miner, Friend of Kings and Queens, Geologist, Conservationist, Oceanographer, and Great White Medicine Man."

When he set out for the West in 1830 to paint the Indian tribes of North America, people warned him it couldn't be done. He'd never come back alive, they said. He'd be butchered by the "savages" before he could set up his easel. But he went nevertheless, and succeeded even beyond his own dreams. After eight hard, dangerous years George Catlin had a pictorial record of Indian life that has never been equalled by anyone.

When his work was done, crowds of people great and small flocked to see "Catlin's Indian Gallery" and to hear the artist tell of his adventures among the Indians. They admired the proud, handsome portraits that hung in rows on the walls. Kings and Princes and great men of many nations paid tribute to him. But few, very few, really listened to what the young artist was saying. To Catlin these were not just pretty pictures to look at. They were real men and women, honorable, kind, good people who—unless white men changed their ways—were doomed to a lingering and cruel death.

In the end, of course, George Catlin's prophesy came true. Yet in his paintings the buffalo still roam, the painted warriors still prepare for battle, the women still guard their cradles, and the great Chiefs still stand in all their finery, gazing out over an unpeopled horizon.

Massacre!

THE RICH, ROLLING, SLEEPY-LOOKING WY-
oming Valley of Pennsylvania had seen bloody warfare
for twenty weary years. Settlers from Connecticut tried again
and again to push the stubborn Pennsylvania farmers off their
fertile lands. But the Pennsylvanians were there first. They
loved their valley and meant to hold on to it, no matter what the
cost. They knew it was theirs by right of a Royal Decree and
also by a fair treaty signed with the Indians. Five times they
fought off the invading Yankees and five times they rebuilt their
towns and homes and farms, and started over again.

Then in the summer of 1778, while the Revolutionary War
was raging to the east, the Connecticut Yankees came again—
this time under the Tory banner and equipped with the best

I

British muskets—and this time they intended to win a decisive victory. With the Tories came a desperate band of Iroquois Indians, half-crazy with the excitement of fighting in a white man's war.

Within days the two main Pennsylvania forts had fallen, and the frightened farmers hastened their women and children to Forty Fort in Wilkes-Barre. Then the men gathered into a makeshift army and marched out to meet the invaders, who outnumbered them three to one.

It was a short battle. Within a few hours the Tories and Indians overran the little army of farmers, and the white flag of surrender was hoisted over the fort.

What followed was sudden and horrible. The gates of the fort burst open; war-whooping Indians stampeded in, trampling and terrifying the women and children. The Tory officers stood by, helpless either to stop the rampage or to allow the prisoners to surrender in a dignified manner.

When it was all over, three hundred men, women and children were dead, and the town of Wilkes-Barre was in flames.

Somehow, little Polly Sutton and her mother escaped, and when the smoke cleared they learned that Polly's father had leaped into the Susquehanna River and swum to safety.

Eleven years after the Wyoming Massacre, Polly Sutton married a Connecticut lawyer named Putnam Catlin. The war was over, Wilkes-Barre was peaceful again, and the massacre was only a distant memory.

As the years passed fourteen children were born to Polly and Putnam Catlin. They grew up listening to their mother's tales of the terror in Wilkes-Barre. The dreaded Iroquis were gone now, having been pushed further to the west, and only a handful remained in Pennsylvania. No one knew much about these survivors, and few white men had seen any Indians in years, or wanted to.

But George Catlin, Polly and Putnam's fifth child, was different. More than anything, he loved to be in the woods, where he could pretend to be an Indian. He would try to move silently along the path, always remembering to stay invisible, and always hoping to meet up with a real Indian.

Born on the 26th of July, 1796, George was only four when Putnam and Polly Catlin packed up their children and belongings and headed north to the little village of Great Bend on the banks of the Susquehanna. George's father had been in poor health. His law practice tired him so much that he had decided to try his hand at farming. There were half a dozen children now, and George and baby James rode the rocky old Mohawk trail on their mother's horse.

The new century was just beginning. The Catlins, like so many other citizens of the new nation, were filled with hope for the future. People everywhere were leaving the towns and heading into the lonely countryside to plant their roots in virgin soil.

The Catlins' journey was only about forty miles long, but they were on the trail many days, riding impatiently behind the plodding ox-carts loaded with axes, rifles, quilts, poultry, tools, law books, pots and pans, and a few good pieces of Connecticut furniture.

Great Bend was such a small settlement that it didn't even have a name at first. Yet the Catlin farm was fertile and beautiful, surrounded by mountains and overlooking the sparkling Susquehanna. Afterwards George remembered his ten years there as the happiest of his life; the place where he learned to hunt and fish, and where he had his first encounter with Indians.

The farm nestled in a valley called the Ouaquagua, which had been the home of woodland Indian tribes since very early times. Each spring, when Putnam Catlin's fields were plowed, dozens of Indian arrowheads, bones and bits of pottery were turned up.

3

The farmhands always put aside these treasures for George, who saved them all. Once they brought him the rusted steel head of a real tomahawk. It was George's prize exhibit.

Each year his "museum" grew larger, and George grew more curious about the vanished men who once had lived and hunted on his father's fields.

In time, George became good friends with the farmhands. During the noonday rest, they told him long tales about the wilderness, and when his father was too busy, they took him fishing. They encouraged him, winking at one another, when he learned to shoot a gun. He was so small, and his old bird gun was so cumbersome, that he had to hold it with both hands. But he was a stubborn lad, and by the time he was nine, he could hit almost any target.

Yet George wasn't satisfied with crows and squirrels. He wouldn't be able to call himself a real hunter until he had shot a deer. His father told him that deer hunting was a man's sport; the boy would have to wait a long, long time.

George didn't want to wait. His two older brothers were away at school, and their big deer rifles, hanging on the kitchen wall, were begging to be used.

The temptation was just too great. It was an easy matter to take one of the big guns and to creep outside in the middle of the night to hide it under some bushes. The boy knew he would be taking a terrible risk, for his father's wrath could be frightful. But all he could think of was how proud his father would be when he dragged home the carcass of a splendid buck. All would be forgiven, and his father would seat George at the head of the table when the venison was served.

Throughout the night and following morning, the rifle lay in its hiding place. George raced through his chores, praying that no one would notice the rifle was gone. At last he found his chance and slipped away, heading for the river with the enormous gun cradled in his arms. Down by an old sawmill, he settled down to wait for his first deer. He had chosen the spot with care. There was a salt lick nearby, and George's brothers had seen many animals here before. Gingerly he braced the long barrel of the loaded rifle in the crotch of a tree overlooking the salt lick.

Suddenly, now that he was actually *here,* looking down the sights of a rifle, George began to tremble. He thought of old John Darrow who had been mauled by a cougar in this very spot. He thought of what might happen when his father discovered what he'd done. And the gun itself: what if it hadn't been loaded right?

Then, as if it had walked right out of George's imagination, a deer appeared in the rifle sights. But the boy was too excited to pull the trigger; before he could control his violent trembling the deer was gone.

George was furious with himself; this time he had missed his chance!

It was growing dark. He would have to go home empty-handed. His father had been right: deer hunting was for men. He was just about to lift the rifle out of its resting place when the deer reappeared—this time much closer.

Almost miraculously, George's trembling stopped. Steadily, he sighted again down the long barrel and his finger found the trigger. It would be a perfect shot.

Bang!!!

The sound came from just behind him and a little to the left. George saw the deer leap up, then fall dead. But his gun was still cocked, the barrel still cold.

Then, out of the underbrush, walked a tall stranger. He strode to the side of the animal and drew a long knife. His red-brown skin gleamed in the dusk and his long black hair shone like coal. There was no doubt in George's mind—it was an Indian.

5

The boy was terrified. He remembered the Wyoming Massacre, and all the fearful tales people told of scalpings and bloody murders. If this Indian, with his huge knife, should see him crouching here, he was lost!

As George huddled in the shadows, trying to hold his breath, the Indian filled his pipe and slowly smoked it. From time to time he looked around him, and George was sure he would be discovered. But at last the stranger put away the knife and, slinging the carcass over his shoulder, he walked away into the trees.

George never looked back. Forgetting the gun, he scrambled up the steep bank, clawing at stumps and rocks, slipping and sliding over the moss. He kept going as fast as he could run, straight across his father's back fields, through brambles and vines and over ditches and fences. Pale as a ghost, he burst into the house, shouting, "I've seen an Indian! I've seen an Indian!"

Breathless, he blurted out his story, but the family could make no sense of it. Indians here? It couldn't be, they said to each other; George's imagination was too active. He's been frightened by some stranger, and he's so enthralled by Indian stories that he's made the whole thing up. But George's mother did believe him and came to his bedroom that night to tell him so. In the morning, when the farmhand, Johnny O'Neil, came around to tell Mr. Catlin there were "gypsies" camped on his meadow, his father exclaimed, "I'll be bound! These are George's Indians."

And sure enough they were. Out on the pasture, George and his father and O'Neil found three strangers huddled under a makeshift shelter, breakfasting on deer meat. Next to the man George had seen in the woods sat his wife and ten-year-old daughter.

Putnam Catlin was, above all, a gentleman. As he always did when strangers turned up in this out-of-the-way spot, he greeted his guests warmly, echoing the man's "how, hows." Soon, though they shared few words in common, they were able to talk together like old friends.

The Indian's name was On-o-gong-way. He had come a long, long way, he said, from Cayuga Lake back here to his boyhood country. While he talked, he passed his pipe to Putnam Catlin and then, with a little smile, to George. The Indian's story was a sad one.

When his parents took him away, he said, they had left behind a pot of gold, and he had returned to find it. Once these fields had been covered with trees and filled with game. Then, after the massacre, everyone had fled. No Indian was safe there any more because the angry farmers were seeking out every last one and shooting them without hesitation.

Years later, George still remembered the Indian's moving speech: "These green fields, my father," said the Indian, looking gravely at Putnam Catlin, "were then the hunting grounds of my fathers, and they were many and strong; but we are now but a very few—we live a great way off, and we are your children."

George listened, spellbound. It was hard to believe that only yesterday George had thought On-o-gong-way might kill him!

The Catlins and their neighbors befriended the little family, brought them gifts and food and spent many hours with them in conversation. George's new Indian friend made him a handle for his rusty tomahawk, and decorated it with strange and beautiful designs. When Johnny O'Neil ground the old blade to a gleaming razor-sharpness, George was happier than he'd been in his life.

But the pot of gold that had brought the Indians here was a bitter disappointment. George's father knew it well, for it had been dug up by one of his plows. It was only a common brass kettle that over many years had grown splendid in On-o-gong-way's memory.

One morning, the Indians were gone. They left behind in the Catlins' woodshed a saddle of venison. Fastened to it was an eagle's feather, a sign of gratitude and friendship.

Several days later, On-o-gong-way's body was found lying in a wild, overgrown valley only a few miles from the Catlin farm. There were two rifle bullets in his chest. After nearly forty years, the Wyoming Massacre had been "avenged" again.

The memory of On-o-gong-way and his fate stayed with George Catlin for the rest of his life. It would be many years before he could understand the full significance of the tragedy, and though he was to witness similar events many times in his life, he would never forget On-o-gong-way or the violence and senselessness of his death.

Putnam Catlin had not taken George's deer hunting escapade lightly. George was ordered to stop wandering into the woods, and there was to be no more gun-shooting. If he knew what was good for him, he would start paying more attention to his lessons.

The boy's father had plans for George. He would complete his schooling in a few years, and then he would go to law school in Litchfield, Connecticut. Then he would return to practice law in Pennsylvania. Putnam was sure he knew what was best for his sons and he expected all of them to follow his guidance and be a credit to the family name. He might be only a farmer now, but he was still a highly educated gentleman. It was not accidental that his neighbors called him "Squire." For a long time he did not notice that George was a dreamer, not a scholar, and it never occurred to him that George might have plans of his own.

The boy struggled hard to live up to his father's expectations. Each day he set off for school on time, clean and bright-eyed. But over and over again he would be delayed by some irresistible distraction: bear tracks on the path, perhaps, or news that the shad were running in the river. More often than not, he got to school late, his ears burning with shame and embarrassment.

When Catlin was a boy, school could be insufferably dull to a bright child like himself. There were few books, and these were choked with heavy sentences that meant little to the child who had to memorize them. "Old Blue Back," the spelling book of the time, contained statements like this: "Language or speech is the utterance of articulate sounds or voices, rendered significant by usage, for the expression and communication of thoughts." "Old Dilworth," the arithmetic book, leaned the other way, trying to make addition and multiplication into a game. But it was a struggle for American students to comprehend pounds, shillings and pence:

> A gentleman a Chaise did buy
> A Horse and Harness too;
> They cost the sum of three Score Pounds,
> Upon my word 'tis true;
> The Harness came to half th' Horse
> The Horse twice of the Chaise;
> And if you find the Price of them,
> Take them and go your Ways.

There was one schoolbook, however, that everyone liked. It was called "Geography Made Easy," and it told of the great world beyond the Appalachians and the Susquehanna, beyond the Atlantic and Pacific. A boy like George Catlin could spend hours with this book, reading about all the races of mankind, their religions, their costumes and their history. And after school, as he fished from a rock at the edge of the Susquehanna, he would have dreamed of Turks and Hindoos and Arabs, of yellow men, black men, red men, living and eating and sleeping —perhaps even fishing—thousands of miles away.

Although school met six days a week, George still found time to get into trouble. When On-o-gong-way had finished the handle of George's tomahawk, he had captivated the boy by the way he could send it whistling through the air, end over end, always landing it perfectly deep in the bark of the tree. After the Indian was gone, George practiced for hours at a time, first throwing it short distances, then gradually lengthening his arc. The other boys in the village begged to try it, too. One day George's best friend missed the target, and the treasured tomahawk glanced off a tree and sliced a deep gash down the left side of George's face. There was no doctor to repair the wound properly, so for the rest of his life he carried the long scar.

In time, George outgrew "Old Blue Back" and carried instead a Latin Grammar bound in leather. But his schoolwork did not improve. As he grew older, he found a new interest to distract him from his studies. Now he not only spent his afternoons prowling the woods; he was also drawing and doodling throughout the school hours.

He drew pictures of his classmates and instructors, and sketched the landscape outside the window. He covered the margins of his papers with drawings, and daydreamed about learning to paint with a brush one day.

His father took a dim view of all this, and lectured him over and over again. Each time George promised to try harder at school, and each time his attention wandered a little farther from the classroom.

When George was about fourteen, his father announced that the carefree days along the Susquehanna were over. Through a business deal, Putnam had acquired some real estate in the town of Hop Bottom and he was taking the family there. To George and his favorite brother, Julius, it was a terrible blow, for it meant leaving the wilderness and becoming "town people." This could only mean more confinement, stricter schoolmasters, more rules and regulations. There would be no possum hunting in Hop Bottom, no fields strewn with Indian arrowheads, and certainly there would be no more playing hooky.

The three Catlin girls were overjoyed with their new friends and the frills displayed at the general store, but the seven boys settled down to "civilized" life with deep regret. George and Julius fretted about their uncomfortable shoes and stiff clothes, and spent innumerable hours planning new ways to slip away to the woods.

Their father seemed not to notice—he was busy practicing law again, buying and selling property, and rapidly becoming a respected member of the community.

In 1811, when George was seventeen, Putnam Catlin was elected to the Pennsylvania legislature. Before he rode off to Harrisburg to assume his new, low-paying duties, he reminded George that it would soon be time to begin his law studies. But as long as he was in the legislature, there would be very little money in the family. Therefore, Putnam had arranged for his son to teach in Hop Bottom's one room school.

Anything would have suited young George better—even plowing fields or haying cows. But no son of Putnam Catlin would be allowed to hire himself out as a common laborer. No, George must work at a profession suitable to an educated gentleman, and teaching it would be.

Dutifully, George Catlin forced himself to go through "Old Blue Black" and "Old Dilworth" all over again. And since his pupils were scarcely younger than he, they doubtless loved him. Certainly his range of interests and his enthusiasm for *real* knowledge—not just the classroom kind—must have delighted them. In any case, his teaching career did not last long. The time for law school finally arrived.

❦❦❦One-room Law School❦❦❦

ON A JULY AFTERNOON IN 1817, GEORGE CAT-
lin climbed down from the stagecoach, and looked around ap-
preciatively at the town where his father had grown up. Litchfield, Connecticut, was a stately town of neat white mansions
set proudly along wide, tree-lined streets. The only movement
was the lazy swaying of the hundred-year-old elms, and the
only sounds came from unseen insects toiling and whirring in
the yards and gardens around the Village Green.

Heading down South Street, as his father had instructed,
George found the home of Judge Tapping Reeve, half-hidden
by trees and flowers and currant bushes.

His knock on the wide green door was answered by Mrs.

Reeve, a huge, smiling woman, and he soon found himself seated uncomfortably in a high-backed wooden chair in Judge Reeve's study. The walls were paneled with wood, and thick, leather-bound books overflowed the shelves onto the tables, the windowsills and even some of the chairs. It was a room where hard work was done, thought Catlin, much like the study in his father's house; a place for deep thought and earnest conversation.

At length the great man arrived. George could see at once that Tapping Reeve was no ordinary person. He was dressed in the fashion of a half-a-century earlier, with a shabby black coat and ancient black shoes buckled like a Pilgrim's over sagging black hose. The Judge's wispy white hair hung to his shoulders, giving him the look of an aged Prophet. He peered vaguely at George as if he had forgotten what he was there for.

George introduced himself politely, and answered the Judge's rambling questions as best he could. Yes, sir, the journey had been a hard one from Pennsylvania. Yes, sir, he intended to work hard at his studies. Yes, sir, his father was in good health. Yes, sir, he was eager to become a good lawyer. Yes, sir, he realized that it was a great privilege to be here.

After a while, the Judge's attention wandered and George took his leave, wondering if this strange, absent-minded, old-fashioned man could possibly teach him anything.

Tucked away in Judge Reeve's garden stood a plain little building twenty-two feet long and twenty feet wide. This, the first law school in America, was about as disappointing to look at as the great Judge Reeve himself.

But the next morning at seven o'clock, when the Judge shuffled into the schoolhouse to begin his lecture, everyone fell silent. In his soft voice, the Judge launched into his customary start-of-the-term remarks. The room was still as the locusts droned in the elms outside the open windows and the Judge talked on. In any other schoolroom on such a day, George Catlin would have found a pencil in his hand and a sketch taking shape on the table before him, but not today. Today, he was completely engrossed in what the old man was saying.

America was a new country—so new that, except for the Constitution, she had almost no laws of her own. The new nation was still making do with the old legal customs of England, the very laws America had fought so hard to be rid of. If the Revolution were not to have been fought in vain, America must examine England's laws and make haste to change whatever was unjust or undemocratic in them. This would be the mission of the Litchfield Law School: to teach not only the technicalities of the law, but also the human principles by which men should govern and be governed.

Tapping Reeve left no illusions in the minds of his students. The course of study would be difficult, and anyone in the room who doubted it might as well leave now.

There would be no textbooks except those in the Judge's study. Therefore, each student would have to write his own. Every morning lectures would be read to the class, which all students were expected to take down *word for word*. In the evening they were to rewrite their notes into thick, bound notebooks. At the end of the course, each student would have five of these volumes, which he could keep and use for the rest of his life. All told, these books would contain more than three thousand pages, and would cover every question and principle of the law, both ancient and modern.

The summer days passed quickly. There were lectures in the mornings, hours of study in the afternoons and discussions of law, politics and life which stretched late into the warm nights. George was determined not to disappoint his father, who had sacrificed so much to send him here. And his father worked equally hard to keep George on the track.

In August, a letter came from Putnam Catlin, with a stern reminder:

You are now placed more favorably for study and the improvement of your mind than you could be at any other place in the United States. . . . Let no temptations whatever allow you to stray from the path of virtue, and strict propriety of conduct. When allurements to vice assault you, instantly think of me, think of home, think of your sisters, your brothers—think of yourself, and you will escape every snare.

While his classmates picnicked away the autumn Sundays, George stuck to his work. When the snows fell, he stayed in his room, studying, while the other young men entertained their ladies at the tavern with a cup of hot rum and a roaring fire. They could well afford to stay two years or more at Litchfield, but word had come from Putnam Catlin that he could not keep George there more than a year.

Finally summer came around again, and George stretched his endurance to new limits, finishing his course and hurrying to Springfield to appear before the strict board of examiners. At last, just after his twenty-second birthday, George Catlin was admitted to the bar, and could call himself a lawyer.

After the stage pulled out of Litchfield and jounced southward toward the Post Road, the young lawyer watched eagerly as the scenery began to change. They passed out of town on wide, shady streets and soon fields of corn and ripening orchards were rolling by. Then, by late afternoon, the road began to climb into the shadowy Berkshire woods. Red-headed woodpeckers drilled in the dusk and families of grouse scattered into the underbrush, startled by the clop of horses' hoofs and the rumble of wheels.

In a week Catlin would be home, free for the first time in more than a year to stalk the birds and ramble in the familiar hills of Pennsylvania. The minute he got home, he would find his brother Julius, who must be all grown up by now. They would pack up some simple food and head into the woods for a little shooting, a little sketching and a fine, long talk like the ones they used to have.

George had had enough of books for a while. Now he would stretch his legs and soak up the sunshine. It would be wonderful!

But he had not reckoned that his influential father would already have lined up his first clients. George's vacation was brief, and all too soon he was back indoors again, practicing his new profession of the law—and struggling with his old urge to cover every available surface with drawings.

In the Luzerne County Court House, the practice of law was far removed from the lofty heights of Tapping Reeve's philosophy. The weeks and months dragged by with never a mention of "inalienable rights" or "justice for all." Instead, Catlin found all his time taken up with petty matters: the collection of debts, the execution of wills, the registration of property deeds. The first man he defended in court was a thief who told Catlin frankly that he was guilty as charged. To the young lawyer's dismay, the judge let the man go free.

Sitting in the courtroom day after day without anything in the way of a real challenge, Catlin began to sketch again. As the judge talked on and on about appellants and judgment creditors and the real estate of the debtors, he was sketching the judge's profile: his nose, his forehead, his chin. The judge finished, he would draw the members of the jury one by one. Then, if it was a particularly long session, there were always the spectators, the witnesses and the notaries.

It wasn't long before drawing became the focus of Catlin's courtroom days. More and more, he was spending his legal fees on sketchbooks and pencils. When he ran out of these, he took out his penknife and decorated the pine table where he sat.

Other young men, like George's brother Charles, were quite

content with the lawyer's life: it brought them an income and a community standing that no other profession could then provide. But such things had never mattered to George. He still wanted to be his own man.

Even Putnam Catlin, stern and rigid as he often was, finally had to admit, after a year or two, that George must be allowed to go his own way.

So George sold his hard-earned, handwritten law books to buy paints, brushes, ivory and canvas, and set off for Philadelphia to become an artist.

G. Catlin, Artist

THE AIR WAS THICK WITH THE FUMES OF turpentine and varnish in George Catlin's little workshop. He laid down the tiny camel's-hair brush he had been painting with and rubbed his burning eyes. When he glanced up at the clock on the mantel, he was surprised to see that it was almost six o'clock. He stumbled to a window and flung it open. A chilly March wind gusted into the room, riffling the piles of sketches on his worktable.

Gratefully, Catlin breathed in the sharp air. Bone-tired, he gazed out of the open window across the slate roofs and tall chimneys of Philadelphia, unaware of the cold gray mist outside. He wasn't thinking about how tired he was, or how cold. He was thinking about success.

18

As an artist, he had made a late start—perhaps too late—for when he arrived in Philadelphia he was more than twenty-five years old. He had never had an art lesson in his life. All he knew about drawing and painting he had learned by himself. And he was a country boy to boot, completely without experience in the ways of a fashionable city like Philadelphia.

Philadelphia was already full of talented and famous painters long before Catlin arrived. There might not be room here for a self-taught artist like George Catlin. But he was sure that if he were to succeed at all, it must be in Philadelphia and nowhere else, for no city in America had higher artistic standards.

Arriving in the city with his paints and brushes and a few simple belongings, George had found lodgings at 116 Walnut Street and put an advertisement in the City Directory: "Catlin, George, miniature painter."

Miniature paintings were all the rage in the 1820's. There were no cameras yet, so people flocked to artists' studios to have portraits painted on little pieces of ivory, often no more than an inch or two wide. Some were designed to be worn on a ribbon around the neck; some went to relatives or sweethearts for keepsakes. Many were displayed on the parlor wall, encased in velvet and framed with gilt. They were lovely little things, and their owners prized them highly. But their size made them extremely difficult to paint.

Before very long, people began to knock on Catlin's door. They looked at his work and liked what they saw. His dark good looks and instinctively gracious manners pleased them, too. Soon they were making appointments to sit for their portraits. Catlin's days became filled with work and his evenings filled with invitations to fashionable parties. The leading artists of the city elected Catlin to the Pennsylvania Academy of Fine Arts—at that time the highest artistic honor in America. George Catlin, artist, had "arrived."

19

But on this chilly March evening, as he stared out over the gray waters of the Delaware River, he was feeling a touch of the old restlessness that used to plague him in the courtroom. What was wrong? He had all the business he could handle. He was known and liked by many important people in the nation's busiest city. He was doing what he loved most—painting—and actually being paid to do it! Yet there was something missing. He still felt he was drifting along without a purpose, without a fixed destination.

His fishing tackle lay tangled and dusty in a corner; his rifle had grown rusty from neglect. And for what purpose? For the sake of a life spent making small pictures of small people? Somewhere, somehow, he had to find a more important, a *bigger* way to spend his life, a way that would absorb all his restless energy.

Up the street, the bell began to ring at Independence Hall. A few blocks away, the bells of St. Joseph's and St. Mary's answered back. It was seven o'clock. His paints were drying out. Time to stop.

Catlin spent many of his evenings at Peale's Museum. For twenty-five cents he could buy a ticket to see Peale's "wonderful works of Nature! and curious works of Art." The ticket admitted him up the handsome staircase of Independence Hall, and into the long, narrow room Charles Willson Peale had crammed with paintings, statues, stuffed birds and animals, fossil bones, Indian spears, reptiles and amphibians pickled in alcohol, and thousands of minerals from every part of the world. It was indeed, as the sign boasted, a "Great School of Nature."

In the evenings, gas illumination (then a novelty) was turned on, organ music was played, and Peale or one of his talented sons would lecture. The subject might be geology, or art, or the solar system, or magnetic currents, or any of the hundreds of subjects that interested the Peales and their fellow Philadelphians.

G. Catlin, Artist

Afterward, Catlin would walk the short distance back to his lodgings and fall asleep listening to the singing and laughter in the cobbled street below. At the foot of the hill, ocean-going ships came and went in the dark. Seamen and stevedores, in search of entertainment at City Tavern, milled about under his window, and he could hear snatches of Portuguese and Italian and Cockney English, half-wishing that he, too, could sign aboard a clipper one day and sail off to some new adventure.

In the end, though, it was not the lure of Macao or Port-of-Spain that finally pulled Catlin away from the genteel life of Philadelphia. George Catlin's destiny, when he finally found it, lay not beyond the oceans, but across a vast sea of grass, thousands of miles overland to the West.

Many years later, Catlin would sit down and write about that destiny in rich detail. It all began in Philadelphia, he wrote. And the idea came to him almost by accident.

One morning, the hubbub in Walnut Street was even livelier than usual. Everyone seemed to be going to a parade: ladies, sailors on liberty, children, servants, dogs, chimney sweeps. They were all talking about a group of Plains Indians who had arrived during the night and set up a camp in back of Independence Hall.

Catlin took the stairs to his room three at a time and, pencil and sketchpad in hand, he raced down to join the crowd heading up the hill. Sure enough, on the wide lawn stood several white tepees, and through the throng of onlookers, he could see that the Indians were like none he had ever met before.

Except for On-o-gong-way, Catlin had known only the miserable, embittered survivors of the Eastern tribes—most of them toothless, drunken, sickly and sullen. They huddled in shacks on the fringes of white men's settlements poaching, stealing, scrounging for an existence.

But these tall, handsome, beautifully dressed men came out

of the vast, unknown plains west of the Mississippi. They didn't cower or cringe or beg like their Eastern kinsmen; they strolled about like royalty. Even in the parlors of Philadelphia, Catlin had never seen such dignity. And the faces! . . . and the richly decorated robes!

The curious crowd jostled his elbows and trod on his feet, but Catlin, sketching the scene before him, didn't notice. He loved the broad lines of the Indian foreheads and cheekbones—so different from the tight lips and pinched expressions of his usual clients. The colors overwhelmed him: rich red-brown skin instead of pasty white; clothing studded with brilliant quills and beads instead of Quaker gray and black. Why, there were colors, here that Catlin didn't even know how to mix!

During the next few days, Catlin sketched and watched the Indians wherever they went. If only he could spend the rest of his life painting *their* portraits!

Of course, that was out of the question. An artist had to make a living like everyone else. Indians would never pay to have their portraits painted. What a ridiculous idea!

Soon the Indians broke camp and headed for Washington City, where the Great White Father in the White House was waiting to meet them. Catlin was left with a few quick sketches —and the beginning of a plan. If Indians could not pay for their portraits, perhaps white men would, if there were enough pictures, and if they were good enough. Here in Philadelphia people paid gladly to see Peale's Museum. After all, old Charles Willson Peale had raised an enormous family partly on the proceeds of his museum of natural history. Why not a Museum of American Indians?

Months went by while Catlin mulled over his idea. He read everything he could about the Indians and the West. Lewis and Clark had met some of the tribes twenty years earlier on their journey to the Pacific. But there were few books to read. Even the maps were mostly blank beyond the Mississippi; only the words "Great American Desert" marked the Indians' home.

The more he studied, the more he realized that he would need money—a great deal of it—before he could start off into this unknown country. He would have to get the permission of the government, too, and letters of introduction to the Indian Agents on the outposts. They and they alone knew where to find the scattered tribes and how to speak to them.

Time passed. Catlin worked even harder on his miniatures, quietly setting aside as much as he could for his future plans.

For a long time, he told nobody about his idea. Who could possibly understand what he had in mind? Not Putnam Catlin, surely, or brother Charles, the lawyer, or brother James, the banker.

Finally, he could keep it to himself no longer; he wrote to Julius. His favorite brother had finished his training at West Point and was now serving as a lieutenant out on the Western frontier at Fort Gibson. Julius really wasn't cut out to be an officer any more than George was cut out to be a lawyer. It was just another notion of their father's that had to be obeyed—for the time being, at least.

From Fort Gibson, Julius replied without hesitation: could he be George's partner? It was the most exciting idea he had ever heard of, to travel the length and breadth of the country collecting portraits and costumes and legends of the Indians. Julius' real passion was geology, and he could paint a bit, too. With his frontier experience he would be a useful guide and traveling companion. If George would let him come along, he'd do anything—anything at all!

Julius' tour at Fort Gibson had many more months to run. But George was glad to wait. In the meantime, his own career was about to take a new turn, and before he could leave for the great West, he would be heading North.

BON-SON-GEE,
KIOWA WARRIOR, *1834*

Thomas Gilcrease Institute

TUNK-AHT-OH-YA,
KIOWA BOY, *1834*

Thomas Gilcrease Institute

National Collection of Fine Arts, Smithsonian Institution

National Collection of Fine Arts, Smithsonian Institution

Thomas Gilcrease Institute

National Collection of Fine Arts, Smithsonian Institution

MAN OF SENSE,
IOWA INDIAN, *1832*

Thomas Gilcrease Institute

NO ENGLISH,
PEORIA INDIAN, *1831*

Thomas Gilcrease Institute

SEMINOLE INDIAN
WOMAN, *1837*

National Collection of Fine Arts, Smithsonian Institution

MICK-E-NO-PAH
1837

National Collection of Fine Arts, Smithsonian Institution

CREEK BILLY,
SEMINOLE INDIAN, *1837*

National Collection of Fine Arts, Smithsonian Institution

Catlin made this pen and ink drawing to serve as the frontispiece illustration for the printed program that accompanied his "Lecture on the Red Indians" at the Indian Gallery.

The Erie Canal

ON OCTOBER 26, 1825, THE ROAR OF A CANNON boomed out over Buffalo, New York, marking the grand opening of the Erie Canal. Miles away down the Niagara River, another cannon answered, then another, and another and another as the waters of Lake Erie moved eastward down the big ditch toward Albany.

It was a momentous occasion. Now, for the first time, Americans could travel quickly and cheaply from New York City to the Great Lakes. At a cost of over $7,000,000, the canal, four feet deep, forty feet wide, and 363 miles long, had been built to carry trade goods to the West and agricultural products to the East.

Thomas Gilcrease Institute

George Catlin was not a tall man—no more than five-feet-nine, at the most. But despite that and despite the old scar on his left cheek, he was as handsome as any young man in Philadelphia. Black-haired and blue-eyed, he always dressed perfectly for his surroundings. Here in the city, he wore a ruffled shirt front. On the prairies, he would travel in buckskins.

As the cannon fire echoed across the state, four gray horses strained at the towropes for a moment, then began to move briskly along the towpath out of Buffalo, pulling the Erie Canal's first boat, the *Seneca Chief,* behind them. Aboard the boat was De Witt Clinton, the man most responsible for this great day, waving to the cheering crowds. With him were politicians and financiers from all over the state, their friends and wives, and a handsome, twenty-nine-year-old painter named George Catlin.

For the next nine days they pioneered the new canal, stopping to drink toasts with crowds of well-wishers who waited at every village. At last, on November 4, Clinton emptied a keg of water from Lake Erie into New York Harbor, and the canal was officially open.

De Witt Clinton was a man of many interests and great power. Catlin had painted miniature portraits of Mr. and Mrs. Clinton, and there had been talk of his painting a full-length portrait of the ex-Governor to be placed in the City Hall in New York.

He was perhaps the most important patron Catlin ever had, for he liked the young artist well enough to introduce him everywhere. It was through De Witt Clinton that Catlin met the political and social leaders of Albany; many of them asked Catlin to paint their portraits, and he soon found that he had more orders than he could handle. Albany delighted him; there were gay parties in the evenings and stimulating people to discover.

Several times Catlin returned to the Erie Canal and traveled back to Buffalo, where the Seneca, Tuscarora and Oneida Indians were living on reservations. These were not the free, independent men of the Plains he yearned to visit, but they would do for practice. He painted their leaders, their derelicts and their outcasts, and stored the paintings away for the day when they would be joined by portraits of their more fortunate brothers.

National Collection of Fine Arts, Smithsonian Institution

Lovingly, with tiny brushes, Catlin captured his bride's beauty and a bit of her mischievousness on a piece of ivory less than three inches square. Of all the hundreds of miniatures he painted, this was one of his finest.

But the artist kept returning to Albany. Perhaps he did not admit it even to himself at first, but the real reason for Catlin's frequent trips to Albany was not so much the well-paying work that waited there (though he needed every penny for his great plan), or even the dances or the society of good friends, much as he enjoyed them. What really drew him back again was a quiet, blue-eyed girl named Clara Bartlett Gregory.

It was a time of high expectations for Catlin in every way. If the present was good, the future looked even better. Julius was free at last, home from the Army, and waiting impatiently to get started for the West. George was confident of his financial position, for his name was becoming better known all the time. So, on one of his visits to Albany, he persuaded Clara Gregory to become his wife.

They were married on May 10, 1828, and George took his bride to New York City, where he had important work to finish. His happiness was boundless. Clara was lovely, she was thoughtful, she was gentle, and she had about her a touch of mischievousness that George adored.

Soon after the wedding, Putnam Catlin wrote his son a letter of congratulation. It contained advice, as his letters always did. But it was advice of a new and pleasant kind: "Take good care of Clara, and love her as much as you please. It is written, 'Thou shalt not worship any graven image,' but it is nowhere written that thou shalt not idolize your wife."

The summer went by in a pleasant haze. George finished a big portrait of De Witt Clinton, and then started on a copy of it for the Franklin Institute in Rochester. Julius was nearby, trying his own hand at miniature painting, and doing well at it, traveling from town to town in New Jersey in search of clients.

Julius was anxious for his brother to finish, for with this commission out of the way, perhaps George would be ready to go in search of Indians. Since his marriage, there had been no talk

Thomas Gilcrease Institute

of the great plan, only a vague promise that they must get together soon.

When George summoned him to New York at the end of the
summer, Julius was sure the time had come. At last, they would
make some definite plans. But as it turned out, all George had in
mind was to ask a favor: would Julius deliver the painting to
Rochester for him?

Ever since his early childhood, Julius had always done whatever his big brother asked him to do, and this time, as always,
he said "yes."

The picture was packed for the journey, and Catlin wished
Julius goodby and good luck, never suspecting that he would
not see his favorite brother and dearest friend again.

One day a letter arrived from Rochester. Out of the envelope
fell a newspaper clipping, dated September 22:

Considerable excitement was produced here by the sudden death of a
young gentleman named Julius Catlin, brother of the celebrated artist
of that name.

He arrived here on Saturday from New York for the purpose of
delivering to the Franklin Institute the portrait of the late lamented
Clinton, painted by his brother for that Institution. On the following
morning he proceeded to the lower falls of the Genesee (at Carthage)

For his first Indian portrait, Catlin selected Red Jacket, one of the
most famous Indians of the time. Painted on the Seneca reservation
near Niagara Falls, it shows the defiant attitude for which the old
orator was known. He had devoted his long life to resisting the ad-
vance of white men—especially missionaries. Of them he said, "These
men know that we do not understand their religion, we cannot read
their Book, they tell us different stories about what it contains. . . .
If they are not useful to the white people, why do they send them to
the Indians? Why do not they keep them home?"

two miles north of this place, for the purpose of taking a sketch of the principle Cascade and the romantic scenery adjacent.

With the object probably of obtaining a full view of the Cataract, he descended the precipitous bank which is nearly 200 feet high, and after taking some sketches on the margin of the river, swam out to obtain a view from the center of the stream leaving his clothes and sketchbook on a rock. A person named Thomas Munn was fishing within a short distance (a rod or two) of Mr. Catlin, says that he swam with much ease, that he was an expert swimmer, but that when a few moments in the water he suddenly shouted, "Help! for God's sake help," and stretching out his hand sunk to rise no more with life . . .

Mr. Catlin was educated mostly, we understand, at West Point, was an intelligent and accomplished gentleman, and proficient in the Arts in which his brother is such a distinguished master. His untimely fate, falling a martyr to his favorite study, in the very rigour of manhood, has created a deep sensation through the village.

Stunned by the awful news, and feeling that he was responsible for it, George grew pale and remote and, finally, ill. Since childhood he had been troubled with a "weak chest." Now it was feared that he had tuberculosis. Clara stood by, helpless to relieve his despair. At last her health, too, began to fail. The loss of Julius not only left George without a brother; it also left him without a plan.

For a year he and Clara wandered about, poor in health and low in spirit. Finding little interest in Washington City, they traveled on to Richmond. In Virginia, Clara was too ill to leave her room in the cheap hotel where they were staying. It is said that Dolley Madison herself, the former First Lady, came and nursed her back to health. George finally landed a big commission in Richmond, and the two stayed on there for several hectic months.

This assignment provided the kind of challenge Catlin needed, and he threw himself into the job. It was to be a grand portrait of the 101 representatives to the Virginia Constitutional

National Collection of Fine Arts, Smithsonian Institution

Catlin said it over and over again; for the Indians, the future spelled "White men—whiskey—tomahawks—scalping knives—guns, powder and ball—small-pox—debauchery—extermination." Big Sail was all too pathetic an example of Indian conditions East of the Mississippi.

Convention. It involved getting portrait sketches of all the dignitaries individually, and then transferring them onto one huge canvas.

The representatives were all pleased with their likelinesses, and if some of them thought the heads and the bodies were poorly matched as to size, it did not dampen their enthusiasm for the finished painting.

Now, like most painters of the day, Catlin was faced with the question of where to go next. He had exhausted the possibilities in Washington and Richmond, and probably Philadelphia as well. Clara was still unwell, but if he took her back to Albany, Catlin would have to return to painting miniatures. This he no longer wanted to do. By their very nature, miniatures were private things, kept close to the heart or next to the hearth. He wanted more than this; he craved a wider audience, a bigger following.

His miniatures were exquisite. Even today, they have a fineness and life that is astonishing. But when he turned his hand to grander things, the results were strangely out of proportion. The heads often seemed too small for the shoulders; after years of miniature painting, the large brushes rebelled in his hand. At thirty-four, George Catlin still had a lot to learn.

There was only one place where he could go to learn these things, where he could choose his own subjects, and where he could hope to make a name for himself as great as the names of Sully, Stuart, Neagle and Peale.

It must have been a hard decision to make, but when his mind was made up, there was no stopping him. As he oiled his guns and stretched his fishing lines his spirits began to rise. He ordered yards and yards of artists' canvas, and new brushes, and a whole rainbow of pigments: blues for the open western skies, reds and browns for the copper skins of his new subjects, and greens for the great stretches of prairies grass that lay ahead of him.

ᔗᔗᔗᔗ Big Fire Boat ᔗᔗᔗᔗ

WHEN THE WHITE MEN CAME TO AMERICA, the Indians met them as friends. It was the Indians who taught them how to get along in the wilderness, how to plant, to fish and to hunt what they needed. The early settlers helped the Indians, too, whenever they could. They all seemed to know that they would have to live together in peace.

No one knows for certain when the friendship began to fall apart. Certainly it happened slowly at first. Every few years more Europeans came to the New World to settle and farm the land. Each group pushed further into the Indians' lands, and soon the Indians were forced to retreat westward to new forests and fields, only to be overtaken in time by still more white men looking for new lands to plow.

45

Indians had no idea of what the white man meant by the word "property." To them, all the land belonged to the Great Spirit. When white men tried to "buy" land from the Indians, the Indians would reply that the land was not theirs to sell.

Europeans couldn't understand this. In their haste to possess the land, they saw only that the Indians were standing in their way. They came to think of Indians as stubborn, stupid "savages," and scorned them for their ignorance.

They began taking the land by force. The Indians tried to fight back, but in the end all but a few were herded away from the lands of their birth and, like cattle, were driven far away to strange, dry, lonely deserts and badlands which no white man wanted.

In 1830, when George Catlin arrived in St. Louis, few people guessed that the story would end this way. There was so much land west of the Mississippi that there must be room to spare for all. But the signs of the inevitable were already there for anyone who could read them.

Because he had helped Meriwether Lewis open the West a quarter of a century earlier, and because he had been for seventeen years the Superintendent of Indian Affairs beyond the Mississippi, William Clark knew more about Indians than most elected officials in Washington City put together. He had met Chief Black Hawk in 1804, and wintered with the Mandans through the blizzards of 1805. In 1806 the Nez Percé had showed him how to feed his starving men on dog meat and moss.

Five years later, James Madison had put Clark in charge of half a continent. He was responsible for keeping the peace from St. Louis to the Pacific, from the Columbia River to the Colorado. In short, General William Clark was king of the "Great American Desert" and all its native inhabitants.

No traveler could venture far into this huge domain without Clark's approval, for his authority was absolute. Raised on

the Kentucky frontier, Will Clark was known for his fairness
—and his toughness.

Clark had spent most of his life listening to the Indians' problems. He tried hard not to turn anyone loose in their territory
who could possibly do them harm, for enough was already being
done by free-lance fur traders. Under French and Spanish rule,
they had been allowed to cheat, lie and steal from the Indians,
and they were still up to their old tricks. Without the government's blessing. Clark could do little to regulate the fur trade,
but he could see to it that land speculators and would-be prof-
iteers of all kinds were firmly turned back at St. Louis.

Apparently George Catlin passed the test. At least, Clark let
the artist accompany him to treaty councils that summer at Fort
Crawford, Wisconsin, and at Prairie du Chien. Here Catlin
was able to get portraits of Sioux, Iowas and several other tribes.
Afterward, Clark let Catlin go wherever he wished, for he saw
that exploitation was the farthest thing from Catlin's mind. In
the fall the artist visited Cantonment Leavenworth and explored
the Kansas River, still getting his bearings and trying his brush
among the Shawnee, Delaware, Kickapoo and Potawatomie.

By the time Catlin headed back up the Ohio River to Pitts-
burgh and took the overland trail to Clara in Albany, he had a
clear idea of what lay ahead. To be sure, Indians could be
found, and painted, at the white man's trading posts, and at
treaty councils. But already many tribes had started inching off
to the west in search of better hunting, and they only came to
the settlements when they had to.

Catlin would have to go West again, and this time he would
be prepared for the dangers and deprivations of the unknown
prairies far beyond the outposts.

In the spring of 1831 he was back in St. Louis. It was still a
small town of crude stone and log houses strung along the bank of
the Mississippi. Everybody knew everybody, and soon, through

friends of friends, Catlin was on his way up the Platte River with Indian Agent John Dougherty in search of new tribes to interview and new faces to paint. As they paddled toward the Rocky Mountains, the artist and the Indian agent became close friends. The more Dougherty told him about the evils of the fur trade, the more anxious Catlin became to complete his work in a hurry; from what the Agent told him, the traders' corrupting influence would put an end to the Plains Indians within a matter of a few years. Like General Clark, Dougherty was helpless to stop the fur trade—in Washington they thought it was essential to the westward expansion—but he spoke out against it whenever he could. On the Platte, there was ample evidence to back up Dougherty's low opinion of the fur trade. It was impossible not to see the change that came over Indians after they had lived a while among the traders; many of the Indians they saw along the Platte were sick, others had given themselves up to cheap whiskey, and almost all had abandoned their beautiful native costumes, having traded all their beaver skins for calico shirts and blankets made in Manhattan.

Catlin wanted to penetrate beyond this hardscrabble frontier. No matter how far he journeyed, "the West" seemed always just a little farther on, just a little beyond his grasp.

Before he left St. Louis in the fall of 1831, Catlin discussed his project with General Clark. Where could the true, brave, independent Men of the Plains be found, and how could an artist from the "civilized" East introduce himself to them?

Catlin's best chance lay with the powerful American Fur Trade Company. Pierre Chouteau, a second-generation trader, was moving forward with a plan that, in its way, was just as ambitious as Catlin's. Chouteau had been voyaging, as his father had before him, far up the Missouri each year to trade with the Indians. For barter, the Fur Company had to transport heavy loads of weapons and cloth and ornaments up the muddy river in crude, unwieldy rowboats. Pierre Chouteau was about to make a gamble: a steamboat called the *Yellowstone,* built to his specifications, had already navigated the Missouri River as far as Fort Pierre. In 1831, it had speeded his trade goods to Indian outposts in record time, and returned to St. Louis before winter —an unheard-of-accomplishment. Now, Monsieur Chouteau was planning to take the *Yellowstone* hundreds of miles farther upriver—to the mouth of the Yellowstone River itself. Catlin urged Monsieur Chouteau to let him come along, but when he returned to St. Louis in the spring of 1832, Chouteau still could not promise the artist a space on the boat.

By the end of April, the steamboat was nearly ready for her Missouri River voyage. Crews of busy workmen raced to put the engines in first-rate running order. Deck hands swarmed the superstructure with paint brushes and polishing rags. Impatient to be off on the spring floods, the fur traders started to load on the goods they hoped to sell to the Indians and trappers far up the river. Finally, Chouteau told Catlin to come aboard.

The *Yellowstone* was an elegant boat, rising high out of the water, her two black smokestacks tall enough to be seen from miles away. The hardy people of St. Louis watched the loading of the *Yellowstone* with some pride and also a little merriment. They made jokes about taking the big steamer up a piece of river which no craft bigger than a rowboat had ever sailed before. It seemed that almost nobody except Monsieur Chouteau believed it was possible to reach the mouth of the Yellowstone with such a boat, let alone continue on farther as Chouteau proposed to do. First of all, people said, he would have to deal with the tricks and surprises of the Missouri River, a river so difficult to navigate that people bragged about it. They called it "the muddiest, the deepest, the shallowest, the bar-iest, the snaggiest, the sandiest, the catfishiest, the swiftest, and the uncertainest river in all the world."

49

On May 9, 1832, the heavily-laden *Yellowstone* pulled out of her berth and steamed into the Mississippi River, her stacks belching black smoke and her side-wheels churning the muddy water. On board was a strange collection of passengers. There was an Indian agent, Major John Sanford, escorting a delegation of weary Assiniboin Indians back to their homelands after a visit to Washington. The rest of the party consisted of a number of hard-living, tobacco-chewing, French-speaking fur traders.

Ahead of them lay at least two thousand miles of hard and dangerous going, for spring rains had undercut the river banks, tossing logs and branches and whole trees into the swift-moving current.

To George Catlin, however, a voyage like this was pure luxury. Accustomed as he was to depending on his own two feet, traveling in a deck chair was an altogether novel experience, so he wasted no time in getting down to work. Even while the last blast of the *Yellowstone*'s steam whistle was echoing across the St. Louis waterfront, Catlin was setting up his easel on deck. They steamed into the Missouri. The city of St. Louis could have been a million miles away. Catlin was headed for the "real" West at last.

When he tired of sketching, he took notes. Everything that interested him was recorded one way or another so that not a minute of the trip would be wasted or forgotten. He had promised to send news of his discoveries to several newspapers back East, and there were letters to be written to his many relatives.

In one letter, Catlin described what happened in the Indian villages when the big steamboat approached:

We had on board one twelve-pound cannon and three or four eight-pound swivels, which we were taking up to arm the Fur Company's fort at the mouth of the Yellowstone, and at the approach to every village they were all discharged several times in rapid succession, which threw the inhabitants into utter confusion and amazement.

Some of them laid their faces to the ground and cried to the Great Spirit; some shot their horses and dogs and sacrificed them to appease the Great Spirit, whom they conceived was offended; some deserted their villages and ran to the tops of the bluffs some miles distant; and others came with great caution and peeped over the bank of the river to see the fate of their chiefs, whose duty it was, from the nature of their office, to approach us, whether friend or foe, and to go on board. Sometimes in this plight they were instantly thrown "neck and heels" over each other's heads and shoulders—men, women and children, and dogs—sage, sachem, old and young—all in a mass, at the frightful discharge of the steam from the escape-pipe, which the captain of the boat let loose upon them for his own fun and amusement.

Each village and tribe, noted the artist, had its own way of explaining the strange, booming, whistling boat. The Mandans called it "the big thunder canoe," and others called it "big medicine canoe with eyes" because they did not know that it was steered by a human being inside the wheelhouse.

The days on the *Yellowstone* passed quickly at first, but as the boat churned on, the scenery gradually became as monotonous as the unceasing drone of the engines and the swish of the paddle wheels. Mile after mile of prairie grass slipped by, day after day, and finally even the captain grew tired of playing pranks on the Indians with his gunpowder and steam. But it was not in Catlin's nature to be bored, and he was always on deck, scanning the shore for signs of wildlife when there were no Indian camps to look at. He saw grizzly bear fishing on the banks, and watched sheep and antelope clambering on the bluffs.

Whenever the captain stopped the ship for fuel or supplies, George was the first to jump ashore for sketches and conversations with the Indians. He met the Sauks and Iowas, Kansas and Omahas, Otos and Sioux, painting many of their chiefs, and making mental notes for the homeward trip when he would be able to return for longer visits.

Pigeon's Egg Head, (Wi-jun-jon) Going to and Returning from Washington, 1832

Scholars now say that the real name of this Assiniboin celebrity was the Light (Ah-jun-jon). But whatever his name may have been, his story was one of Catlin's favorites. On the left, Catlin painted the brave warrior as he looked leaving his village in 1831, to visit the Great White Father in Washington. On the right, he is seen returning a year later on the *Yellowstone*. He wore a snappy blue uniform given him by the President, with umbrella, fan, and whiskey bottles added by himself to show how worldly he had become. Catlin traveled with him up the Missouri and watched, amused, while he tried to re-establish contact with his family and friends. It wasn't a success. At first they pretended not to recognize him. Then the man's wife cut up his new finery to make an outfit for herself. She made a garter out of his flashy hatband, and leggings out of his regimental breeches. After his kinsmen had endured his stories of the "big city" a few hundred times, they finally killed him for a braggart and a liar.

Thirteen hundred miles above St. Louis, the *Yellowstone* put in for provisions at a Poncah village on the west bank of the Missouri, and the artist was glad to get off and stretch his legs. Fascinated, he watched the scene spread out before him, for it was moving day. The whole village was getting ready for a long journey to the western prairies in search of buffalo. Everywhere the Indians were rushing about, collecting their simple possessions. At a signal from the chief, the wigwams were taken down, folded, and lashed to the poles on which they would be carried. Parents rounded up their children and dogs, and at another signal assembled for the departure.

Just then Major Sanford, the Indian agent, nudged the artist's elbow and pointed to the edge of the clearing. There, on a tattered buffalo skin, lay an Indian who would not make the trip. It was an old, old man, once a great chief, but now too old and sick to travel. Catlin was horrified; to him it seemed unbelievably cruel to abandon the old man to the wind and weather and wolves.

"I am old," said the man, "and too feeble to march. Our nation is poor, and must go to the country where there is meat. My eyes are dimmed and my strength is no more; my days are nearly all numbered, and I am a burden to my children; I cannot go, and I wish to die."

Taking a last leave of his children, he said, "Keep your hearts stout, and think not of me; I am no longer good for anything."

At the end of this simple ceremony, the Indians departed, leaving the old man and the artist alone. Knowing that he was the last person likely to see the old chief alive, Catlin shook hands with him, and with heavy feet turned back to the bank of the river, where a skiff was waiting to carry him to the *Yellowstone.*

Now the *Yellowstone* was heading into trouble. A few days upriver from the deserted Poncah village, the ship ran aground on a sand bar. For a full week she lay there while captain and crew searched the sky for the rain clouds which would rescue them. But the sky remained clear, the ship's keel rested firmly on the bottom.

As each day passed, Catlin grew more restless. The traders, too, were itching to be on their way, and were beginning to grumble. The Indians, miserable at the long confinement they had already endured on board, lapsed into sullenness.

One day word reached the captain that at least a thousand Sioux were encamped up ahead, at the mouth of the Teton River, waiting to see the famous "thunder canoe." The traders, hearing this, insisted on proceeding by land rather than wait any longer for rain. Twenty of them announced that they would leave the ship and head for the encampment on foot.

Naturally, Catlin begged to come with them, but the traders warned him in their colorful language—part-French, part-English, part-profanity—that the march would be too much for a city man. Catlin could see nothing but soft, waving prairie grass ahead. It looked as though they would be walking on clouds. At last, seeing how eager the artist was, the traders relented.

They strode off into the high grass and headed for the horizon. They waded waist-deep through black-eyed susans, purple clover, orange butterfly-weed, wild peas, and oceans of grass; silvery grass, green grass, brown grass, red grass—grass, grass, grass. From time to time, they startled a family of prairie chicken or a swarm of sky-blue butterflies. But the sky stayed the same, the warm sun stayed the same, the same west wind pounded at them across the prairie, and the same grass stretched in front of them all the way to the same flat horizon.

Nevertheless, the artist trudged doggedly on, his sketchbook slung over his back and his rifle in his hand. Every painful step brought him closer to the great Sioux encampment, but try as he might to keep up, Catlin fell farther and farther behind the group. Like the rest of the party, Catlin was wearing only soft-

55

soled Indian moccasins, and like all city people, he had been walking with his toes turned out. The pain in his feet had become intolerable, and he was sure he could go no further. A wise half-breed Canadian, sent back to find the straggling artist, discovered the problem at once, and gave Catlin a lesson in walking he was never to forget.

"Simply turn your toes in as the Indians do," he said in French.

The change was miraculous, wrote Catlin. "I soon found that by turning my toes in my feet went more easily through the grass, and by turning the weight of my body more equally on the toes I soon got relief, and made my onward progress very well. I rigidly adhered to this mode, and found no difficulty on the third and fourth days of taking the lead of the whole party, which I constantly led until the journey was completed."

The little group passed huge herds of buffalo, which supplied them with food. At last, far in the distance, they saw a range of blue hills. It was the first landmark they had seen in many days of endless, flat, unchanging horizons, and the weary men hailed it with joy.

Bone-tired, with Catlin still in the lead, the party arrived at Fort Pierre, on the mouth of the Teton River. All around the little log trading post Catlin could see the tall white wigwams of the Sioux.

By now, Catlin had a well-tested system for gaining the confidence of the Indians. Here at Fort Pierre, as usual, the artist introduced himself to the chiefs, and after the customary exchange of compliment and flattery, he launched into his standard speech.

He spoke at length of the "white chiefs" far away to the East. These chiefs, he said, waited eagerly to see pictures of the great leaders of the West. He told them of the great hardships he had borne for the sake of painting such pictures. Then, dramatically, he unrolled a number of his best portraits, which he always carried with him for this purpose. As always, the Indians marveled at Catlin's work. Surely Catlin must have some magic power, they thought, to be able to paint so realistically. They crowded around eagerly, praising the skill of this "great white chief and medicine man."

Catlin knew it was time to get started with his work, and he invited the chiefs to come into the fort to have their portraits made. But he didn't move fast enough. Already, the medicine men were circulating around the camp, warning the tribesmen not to submit to any magic. They predicted bad luck and even death for any Indian unwise enough to let the mysterious stranger "take away" his face. The women began moaning and crying to show their fear. It looked as though here, among the magnificent Sioux, after a grueling two hundred-mile march, Catlin might lose the opportunity of a lifetime.

He had no choice but to fight suspicion with flattery. Privately, he arranged a talk with Chief One Horn. He mentioned the chief's bravery, his wisdom, his fame as a warrior, his great leadership, his fine face and figure. Surely such a brave and famous chief deserved to have his portrait shown to the brave and famous white "chiefs" in the East.

One Horn could hardly turn down such an honor, and allowed Catlin to paint his portrait.

The painting complete, Catlin hung it outside the fort for all to see. Then he brought the chief himself before the curious crowd, to prove that One Horn was still alive and well. One Horn spoke to his people, telling them that the experience was quite painless after all. He called Catlin a great "Ee-cha-zoo-kah-ga-wa-kon, or "medicine painter," who had come a long way to see the people and to smoke with them. If they posed for him, he promised, no harm would come to them.

One Horn's speech undid much of the damage done by his

57

medicine men, and scores of braves returned to their wigwams to dress for their portraits.

After he had finished with the leading braves, Catlin proposed to paint some of the women as well. This was a huge joke to the Sioux. What a mistake, they cried, to waste time painting the lowly squaws, who had never taken a scalp or done anything more notable than dressing skins and building fires!

The situation called for a tactful solution, and fortunately the artist was prepared. He only wanted the pictures of the women, he explained, to show how they looked and dressed. Of course, he would hang their portraits *below* those of their husbands, when he showed them to the eastern chiefs. Satisfied, the men allowed Catlin to proceed.

He had to work long into the night at Fort Pierre, because he often had to make two copies of each painting: one for his growing collection and one for the Indians to keep. "The vanity of these men," he wrote, "was beyond all description, and far surpassing that which is oftentimes immodest enough in civilized society. An Indian often lays down from morning till night in front of his portrait, admiring his own beautiful face, and faithfully guarding it from day to day to save it from accident or harm."

Gradually, the Sioux lost some of their self-consciousness, and Catlin was allowed to paint their ceremonies and rituals. He was just finishing an exciting picture of the Sioux scalp dance when, from the river below the fort, he heard the all-too-familiar sound of cannon fire, and shortly the *Yellowstone* chugged into sight, none the worse for her long ordeal on the sandbar. Fort Pierre was only the midpoint of Monsieur Chouteau's proposed route, and he urged his passengers to get aboard without delay. Indian farewells, however, could not be rushed, and it was not until the following morning that the steamer could resume the voyage.

Fort Union

THE *YELLOWSTONE* COULDN'T HAVE AR-rived at a better time. Catlin was in serious trouble among the Sioux, and he had stretched his luck just about as far as it would go. Mr. Laidlaw, manager of the fort, had brought Catlin a young brave named the Little Bear, thinking he would make a fine portrait. Catlin, delighted with the man's war dress, started painting him immediately, just as he stood, looking off to the side. While he was at work, he noticed one of the lesser chiefs, the Dog, watching intently over his shoulder. At last, in a sarcastic voice, the Dog remarked to Little Bear, "I see that you are but half a man."

"Who says that?"

59

At Fort Union, Indians of many tribes gathered from hundreds of miles away, and often tempers flared. While Catlin was there, a shooting occurred; one of the Crees mortally wounded one of the Blackfeet. The Blackfeet summoned their medicine man, but to no avail. Despite his efforts, the victim died.

"I say it; the white medicine man knows that one-half of your face is good for nothing, as he has left it out of the picture."

Little Bear replied, "Let the *painter* say it, and I will believe it; but when the Dog says it, let him *prove* it."

The Dog left in a huff, and Little Bear, saying nothing, continued to pose until Catlin finished the portrait. Then he went to his tent.

Some time later, the Dog appeared outside Little Bear's tent with a gun. He challenged the brave to come out and prove what kind of man he was. As Little Bear rushed out there was a sound of shots, and in an instant the young brave was lying on the ground, the "good for nothing" side of his face completely shot away.

The Sioux, in an uproar, went for their guns—some to defend the Dog, and some to avenge Little Bear's death.

"Now we shall have it!" cried Laidlaw to his guest. "That splendid fellow, the Little Bear, is dead! The devil take pictures! I have been afraid of them. I have urged these people to sit for these pictures, and they are saying everywhere that you are the cause of the Little Bear's death. The warriors of the Little Bear's band are all arming, and, if they can't kill the Dog, they have said they will look to you for satisfaction."

Thus it was that Catlin found the thunder of the *Yellowstone*'s cannon one of the sweetest sounds he had ever heard. As the big steamer sped upriver, each hour brought the artist closer to safety. Soon they were far beyond the range of any Sioux war party, and Catlin was on deck again, sketching the strange and beautiful landscape of the Missouri plateau.

By the fifth of June, when the ship finally reached Fort Union at the mouth of the Yellowstone River, St. Louis, the place Catlin called "home" was two thousand miles behind him. This was a different world.

"The finest specimens of Indians on the continent are in these regions!" exulted the artist in a letter to New York. There were

Ojibwas, Assiniboins, Blackfeet, Crows, Cheyennes and Mandans milling about the fort in large numbers, trading with one another and with the men from the *Yellowstone*.

Kenneth McKenzie, the agent of the American Fur Company, was an adventurer and explorer in his own right. He turned one of the fort's bastions over to Catlin, who set up a studio there at once, using a twelve-pound cannon for a chair.

This time, the artist immediately found himself surrounded —almost suffocated—by curious Indians, and the response to Catlin's standard speech was so enthusiastic that the chiefs of the various tribes had to place guards at his door, spears in hand, to keep back the crowds. And the chiefs themselves began to select the lucky notables who would be allowed into the artist's "medicine room."

The atmosphere at Fort Union was already tense. Many of the tribes gathered here were sworn enemies from time immemorial. They were only together from necessity, to trade with the American Fur Company. Mr. McKenzie always took away their weapons when they came to Fort Union, but when their trading was done, they were free again to fight.

When Catlin arrived the situation grew dangerous, for everyone wanted to be painted. Privately, the artist worried about "these wild and jealous spirits, who all meet here to be amused and pay me signal honors, but gaze upon each other, sending their sidelong looks of deep-rooted hatred and revenge around the group."

Despite the rivalry among the tribes, Catlin produced some of his finest work at Fort Union. Seated "on the cool breech of a twelve-pounder," he painted from dawn to dark and sometimes long into the night.

My painting-room has become so great a lounge and I so great a "medicine-man" that all other amusements are left, and all other topics of conversation and gossip are postponed for future consideration. The chiefs have had to place "soldiers" (as they are called) at my door, with spears in hand, to protect me from the throng, who otherwise would press upon me, and none but the worthies are allowed to come into my medicine apartments, and none to be painted except each as are decided by the chiefs to be worthy of so high an honor.

Here were "undoubtedly the finest looking, best equipped, and the most beautifully costumed [Indians] of any on the Continent. Amongst and in the midst of them am I, with my paint pots and canvas!"

Catlin had never worked so hard, and never enjoyed himself more. In the urgency and excitement of recent weeks, the artist was losing his self-consciousness along with his city ways. He found that he no longer had to struggle with proportion and perspective; the faster and harder he worked, the more closely his hand obeyed his eye. To vary his days, he took long rides into the surrounding countryside, sketching the scenery and daily occupations of Indians he met along the way.

Catlin stayed on at Fort Union long after the *Yellowstone,* belching and whistling, set off on her homeward journey. When his work was done, the artist would ride the river currents home in a canoe. Meanwhile, there was so much to do and admire here that for a while the artist lost all track of time.

Here he watched his first "medicine dance" and was so impressed by the Blackfoot medicine man's costume that he parted with a good share of his money to buy it for his collection. This outfit was made from the skin of a yellow bear—strange enough in that region—to which were attached, he wrote, "the strangest mixture, perhaps, of the mysteries of the animal and vegetable kingdoms that ever was seen . . . the skins of snakes, and frogs, and bats—beaks and toes and tails of birds—hoofs of deer, goats, and antelope; and, in fact, the 'odds and ends' and fag ends, and tails, and tips of almost everything that swims, flies, or runs, in this part of the wide world."

This extraordinary costume would be one of his finest exhibits one day, hoped the artist. He also bought here a costly

63

National Collection of Fine Arts, Smithsonian Institution

Buffalo Chase:
The Surround, *1832*

🌀 Recipe for Pemmican
Sun-dried buffalo meat, sliced thin;
buffalo fat; marrow grease; dried
unpitted black cherries (optional).

Pulverise meat in rawhide mortar
with stone pestle. Melt fat and grease
and stir in to taste. Crush cherries
with pits; add as desired. Pack in hide
sacks. Store until later.

Calories: 3500 per pound.
Average serving: ¾ pound daily.

but beautiful Crow tepee made of buffalo skins dressed to a pure white. It stood twenty-five feet high, and was richly ornamented with scalplocks and vivid paint. Large enough for forty men to dine under, it, too, would amaze the people back East.

Besides his collection of costumes and artifacts, Catlin was also adding to his growing museum of Indian portraits. He painted the tall, white-clad Crows, the stocky, dark-clothed Blackfeet, the Assiniboin "stone-boilers," and the "pretty and pleasant" Crees.

The longer he stayed, the deeper grew Catlin's admiration for these proud people. The better he came to know them, the less he thought of them as "curiosities," for he was beginning to join in their lives as a brother. And yet he looked at them with sadness, for he knew what they did not know: that their independence and their freedom was not to last much longer. They enjoyed the finest horses on the Continent and the most abundant game. Their hunting grounds seemed to be un-limited. But the white fur traders had already arrived among them with their diseases, their whiskey and their worthless trinkets. And behind the traders would soon come a much larger and more powerful group—the settlers, the squatters, the miners, the sod-busters, the sheep-ranchers. Already news was reaching the crowded East that there were vast, unfenced, fer-tile lands out West to be had for the taking. Catlin knew noth-ing could be done to stop the oncoming rush. He could already see in his mind the Indian's final destruction at the hands of the white man, and sensed that its time was not far off. At least Catlin could preserve the image of these magnificent people on his canvas and in his sketchbooks. Later, when it was all over, the world might some day see what had been lost.

Even the buffalo might not last, he supposed. At the time there were so many buffalo that one could sit in a single spot all day long watching the herds move by, and at the day's end there would still be more approaching. But the traders were offering fantastic prices for buffalo robes. It was becoming common for a party of Indians to slaughter hundreds of buffalo in a single hunt—not for food, but simply for the hides. The carcasses would be left in fields for the wolves to finish off. How long could the great herds survive such wasteful killing?

One day, Kenneth McKenzie announced that the fort's meat supply was running low. It was time to bring in more, and as a good-sized herd of buffalo had been sighted near the fort, all the men, Catlin included, were to mount horses and see what they could bring in. It was Catlin's first buffalo hunt, and he started out in a high state of excitement. The men stripped off all unnecessary clothing and stuffed their pockets and even their mouths with bullets. They approached the buffalo downwind but soon, as expected, the buffalo saw them and began to charge around in blind confusion. Catlin soon became separated from the rest of the party, but, determined to succeed, he picked out the biggest buffalo he could find and fired. For a moment, Catlin was swept away in the trampling herd, his breath sucked out of his mouth by the whirling dust. The big bull was only wounded, though, and he turned on poor Catlin with such a ferocious expression that the artist forgot all thoughts of hunting and whipped out his sketchbook. The bull stamped and snorted and tried to attack. Failing that, he tried to terrify the artist with his murderous eyes. Catlin could easily have finished off his prey with a single shot, but he was so fascinated by his first close-up look at such a beast that he kept his horse within inches of the thrashing bull until he had sketched him from every possible angle.

When the rest of the party returned, Catlin was in for a good bit of teasing. First of all, they said, he had picked a creature so old and tough that not even the wolves would eat his meat. But what was really funny to them was the idea of riding horseback amidst stampeding buffaloes with paper and a pencil. Catlin must be out of his mind!

National Collection of Fine Arts, Smithsonian Institution

The head chief of the Blood tribe was "a good looking and dignified Indian, about fifty years of age, and superbly dressed." His pipe was richly decorated with porcupine quill designs, and his deerskin shirt was fringed with hundreds of locks of black hair from the scalps of his enemies.

Catlin took the joshing good-naturedly. He was exhilarated by the whole occasion, and though he had not added to the American Fur Company's meat supply, he had sketches that would inspire scores of dramatic paintings in the future. His paintings of the buffalo would join the paintings of the Indians as records of a lost, glorious time in American history.

It was now July, and time to make preparations for the long canoe trip downriver. From the *Yellowstone* Catlin had spotted many villages yet to be visited, and though there was enough to occupy him for months at Fort Union, there was not much time to lose if he was to make it back to St. Louis by winter.

Catlin was not usually a worrier—if he had been one to put caution first, he would never have come this far. But now one thing bothered him more than a little. Where could he find a companion for the return voyage?

It would be a long and difficult trip. From the deck of the *Yellowstone* Catlin had seen enough shoals in the river and grizzly bears on shore to know he should not make the trip alone. Fort Union had its share of trappers and traders, and Catlin had met them all. But few were the kind of men Catlin would trust with his life, and of these few, none were the sort he wanted to spend four or five months with in the confinement of a birchbark canoe.

Then one day, on one of his rides out of the fort, Catlin was approached by a party of trappers on horseback. At its head rode a "dauntless, semi-barbarian looking, jolly fellow," and as they talked, Catlin knew he had found his man.

Catlin was so delighted by his first conversation with Ba'tiste that he wrote it all down that night. It was the first of countless weird, funny, impossible-sounding exchanges that would pass between them in the months to come. Catlin spoke first:

"What distance are you," asked Catlin, "west of Yellowstone here, my good fellow?"

Royal Ontario Museum, Toronto

BUFFALO HERD GRAZING, *1857*

Catlin studied the buffalo from many angles. Here, he followed the Indian practice of hiding beneath the skin of a wolf. Though he became an expert buffalo hunter, Catlin often preferred to let the Indians do the hunting.

Thomas Gilcrease Institute

"Comment?"

"What distance?"—(pause)—"quel distance?"

"Pardon, monsieur, je ne sais pas, monsieur."

"Ne parlez vous l'Anglais?"

"Non, monsieur, I speaks de French and de Americaine; mais je ne parle pas l'Anglais."

"Well, then, my good fellow, I will speak English, and you may speak Americaine."

"Pardon, pardon, monsieur."

"Well, then, we will both speak Americaine."

"Val, sare, je suis bien content, pour I see dat you speaks putty coot Americaine."

"What may I call your name?"

"Ba'tiste, monsieur."

"What Indians are those so splendidly dressed, and with such fine horses, encamped on the plain yonder?"

"Ils sont corbeaux."

"Crows, ha?"

"Yes, sare, monsieur."

Thomas Gilcrease Institute

Setting off to war in "Indian File," or fishing for spotted trout under a waterfall, Catlin saw and admired the rhythm of Indian life, and put that rhythm in his work.

"We are, then, in the Crow country?"

"Non, monsieur, not putty exact; we are in de contrae of de dam pieds noirs."

"Blackfeet, ha?"

"Oui."

"You live here, I suppose?"

"Non, monsieur, I come fair from de West."

"What, from the West? Where under the heavens is that?"

"Wat, diable! de West? Well, you shall see, monsieur, he is putty fair off, suppose."

"You are in the employment of the American Fur Company, I suppose?"

"Non, monsieur, not quite exact; mais, suppose, I am 'free trappaire'; free, monsieur, free."

"Free trapper—what's that?"

"Well, monsieur, suppose he is easy pour understand—you shall know all. In de first place, I am enlist for tree year in de Fur Comp in St. Louis, et I have come de Missouri up, et I am trap castors [beavers] putty much for six years, you see, until I am learn very much; and den you see, Monsieur McKenzie is give me tree horse; one pour ride, et two pour pack (mais he is not buy, him not give, he is lend), and he is lend twelve trap; and I have made start into de Rocky Mountaigne, et I am live all alone on de leet rivares pour prendre les castors, et Monsieur McKenzie is give me coot price pour all."

"So Mr. McKenzie fits you out, and takes your beaver off you at a certain price?"

"Oui, Monsieur, oui."

"Well, you must live a lonesome and hazardous sort of life; can you make anything by it?"

"Oui, oui, monsieur, putty coot, mais if it not pour de dam rascalité Riccaree, et de dam pieds noirs, de Blackfeet Ingin, I am make very much monnaie, mais I am rob—rob—rob too much."

"What! Do the Blackfeet rob you of your furs?"

"Oui, monsieur, rob, suppose, five time! I am been free trappaire seven year, et I am rob five time—I am something left not at all—he is take all; he is take all the horse—he is take my gun—he is take all my clothes—he is take de castors—et I am come back with foot. So in de fort, some cloths is putty much monnaie, et some whisky is give sixteen dollares pour gall; so you see I am owe de Fur Comp six hundred dollares, by gar!"

"Well, Ba'tiste, this then is what you call being a free trapper, is it?"

"Oui, monsieur, 'free trappaire'—free!"

"Have you been robbed this time, Ba'tiste?"

"Oui, monsieur, by de dam pieds noirs—I am loose much; I am loose all—very all—eh, bien—c'est le dernier fois, monsieur. I am go to Yel Stone. I am go le Missouri down. I am go to St. Louis."

Catlin made his proposal on the spot. Would Ba'tiste come with him to St. Louis?

"Oui, monsieur," he would, with pleasure.

Beaver Tails & Buffalo Tongues

ON A FINE MORNING IN MID-JULY, CATLIN said goodby to all his friends at Fort Union. His canoe was filled to the gunwales with canvases, paints, ammunition, and Indian dresses. For food, there was a supply of beavers' tails and dried buffalo tongues. For cooking, there were three tin cups, a kettle, a plate and a frying pan. Ba'tiste, the French Canadian, took the bow. Abraham Bogard, a vacationing trader from Mississippi, sat in the middle, and the artist took the steering oar in the stern. As they guided the heavy craft into the river's current, a cheer went up on the bank, where everyone was lined up to watch their departure. The current soon had the canoe moving briskly downstream, and in a few minutes Fort Union was out of sight.

The mud and silt of spring had settled now; the river was

75

clear and sparkling. The fantastic clay cliffs along the Missouri's banks looked even more spectacular from the little canoe than they had from the decks of the big steamboat. "The whole country," he wrote in his notes, "seemed to have been dug and thrown up into huge piles, as if some giant mason had been there mixing his mortar and paints, and throwing together his rude models for some sublime structure of a colossal city!!!"

They did not make the smoothest possible start. Almost at the outset, the kettle went overboard. Attempts to make coffee in the frying pan were "a decided failure," so Bogard, who adored coffee, had to make do with coffee grounds and sugar served from his pocket.

For the first few days the three enjoyed the silence of the river, the beauty of the scenery and the pleasant motion of their paddles through the water. Then one morning, before dawn, they woke up to find gazing at them a grizzly bear and her cubs. The bears had already eaten every scrap of food in the canoe, and untied and inspected all of the baggage. Paint powders, ripped from their packages, were mingled on the sand like a rainbow gone mad. Catlin, who knew better than to stand up, reached for his rifle and pistols. But Ba'tiste, just then, spotted the father of the family approaching. Very carefully, so as not to anger the bears, but as fast as possible, Catlin and his companions made for the canoe and headed for the middle of the river. All day Ba'tiste and Bogard told hair-raising bear stories, and though they talked bravely of their exploits they paddled harder than usual, and didn't stop for breakfast until five in the afternoon.

Now that they were more than a hundred miles from the protection of Fort Union, it was wise to take greater precautions. The three would cook their evening meal and enjoy the lingering sunset as usual, but then instead of curling up into their robes for the night, they were careful to slip a good distance downstream from the campfire to avoid surprise attack. Since

76

the bears had finished off the food, they now depended on the delicious wild fruit to be found along the banks, and on the small animals and birds they were able to shoot from time to time. Once, the artist had his finger on the trigger and was about to shoot what he thought was a big elk, thinking happily of the many meals it would provide. But just in the nick of time, he realized that the "elk" was an Indian pony, and that nearby was a war party of Arikaras. This time, the canoe put off from shore so fast that Catlin nearly was left behind to face a very serious situation. Fighting the swift current, Ba'tiste and Bogard managed to swing back and pick up their embarrassed employer. The Arikaras were to be avoided at any cost!

The canoe made rapid progress, despite frequent stops for hunting and painting. Soon, high on a bluff, they made out the curious roofline of the Mandan village at Fort Clark. Of all the places Catlin hoped to visit, this was the most crucial to his work. A great deal would depend upon his reception here.

A white man, to reach this village, must travel by steamboat—by canoes—on horseback and on foot; swim rivers—wade quagmires—fight mosquitoes—patch his moccasins, and patch them again and again, and his breeches; live on meat alone—sleep on the ground the whole way, and think and dream of his friends he has left behind; and when he gets here, half-starved, and half-naked, and more than half sick, he finds himself a beggar for a place to sleep, and for something to eat.

It was July, 1832. When George Catlin wrote these words he had been away from his wife, his family and friends for months. His thirty-sixth birthday was only a few days off, and for a moment he felt a chill of doubt. Was it right to do what he was doing? Would his work really accomplish anything? Would "the cits"—the people in the cities back East—ever be able to understand what he was trying to tell them?

77

BIRD'S-EYE VIEW OF THE MANDAN VILLAGE, *1832*

The Medicine Lodge (center foreground), larger than the others, was to be the scene of the religious ceremonies. Beyond the thick-walled earth lodges and the stockade, Catlin could see the burial ground where the dead were laid to rest on platforms. The Missouri River flowed by at the right; the American Fur Company's Fort Clark was a short distance inland at the left.

CATLIN PAINTING
THE PORTRAIT
OF FOUR BEARS

CATLIN FEASTED
BY THE MANDAN CHIEF

Four Bears, second chief of the Mandans, was the most popular man of the village. He welcomed the white stranger warmly, and Catlin painted his friend many times. These two pictures were painted more than thirty years after his visit to Fort Clark. At the top, Catlin is painting Four Bears' portrait while the villagers look on, covering their mouths in astonishment. Below, Four Bears entertains the artist at a feast of buffalo ribs, pemmican and wild turnips.

Here he was in the "strangest place in the world," the village of the Mandans, outside the walls of Fort Clark. He had been welcomed warmly by James Kipp and the other traders at the fort. But the Mandans were another matter. Like most of the tribes along the Upper Missouri, the only white men they ever saw were traders. These traders had often lied to them, cheated them and treated them with contempt. Why, then, should they trust Catlin, who was, after all, only another white man?

Catlin knew from experience that the Indians would need time to get used to him, so he took his sketchbook and climbed to the roof of one of the large, dome-shaped lodges to observe the life of the village below him. Swallows swooped past his ears, and butterflies drifted by. His tired eyes took in the cheerful bustle of the village, and as the sun eased the ache in his body, he began to feel his old enthusiasm return. Around him were almost a hundred other round lodges, each the home of fifteen or twenty people. The earthen roofs were strewn with buffalo skulls, bright cloth, baskets, boats and pottery. On tall poles outside the lodges waved scalps, shields and other trophies of war. Swarming over the doomed roofs and between the lodges were babies, mothers, maidens, old men, and handsomely dressed youths all laughing and talking and playing games. To Catlin, the scene was irresistible. With Mr. Kipp to translate for him, he was soon strolling around the village chatting easily with everybody, his dark mood forgotten. It would be many days before he became aware of the other side of the Mandans' seemingly carefree world.

Catlin was deeply impressed by the kindness and generosity of these people. They gladly shared with him not only their food but their stories and jokes. Before he knew it, the Mandans had made Catlin feel at home—more so than any other tribe he had visited. Soon they were showing Catlin how to take a steam bath, and how to swim overhand, as they did, in the cool water of the Missouri below the bluffs.

And here in the Mandan village Catlin found a man who was to be one of the closest and dearest friends he would ever have: Four Bears, the second chief. Catlin spent many happy evenings feasting and talking in Four Bears' lodge. They had a great deal to discuss, these two, for Four Bears was not only a fine conversationalist, but he was also an artist in his own right. The beautiful robes he wore were all painted by his own hand, and he wanted Catlin to give him some instruction. So after a fine meal of buffalo stew, and a good smoke from the chief's three-foot pipe, they would take whatever materials came to hand—lumps of charcoal from the fire, perhaps—and the drawing lesson would begin.

Though he slept inside the fort, Catlin was seldom there. As soon as the sun was up, he headed for the Mandan village. At that hour, the prairie dogs were gobbling their breakfast of grass seeds, and the avocets were swooping over the river on pointed, multicolored wings. Catlin stayed at his easel for hours at a time, painting portraits of men, women and children. He was fascinated by the unusual coloring of these particular Indians: instead of the straight black hair and dark eyes of all the other tribes, the Mandans were often blue-eyed and gray-haired. Surely there was some explanation; perhaps the Mandans were not Indians at all, but descendants of some unknown European ancestors.

If the Mandans knew anything of their early history, they kept it to themselves. But for the moment, Catlin was occupied with a still deeper mystery. In the center of the village stood one lodge which was far larger than all the rest. Catlin knew this was the "medicine lodge" but not even Four Bears would tell him much about how this lodge was used. In the last few days, Catlin had been noticing a growing amount of activity there. Men were constantly coming and going from its door, intent on duties Catlin could not interpret. When he asked Kipp about it, the answer was a curt, "Wait and see."

National Collection of Fine Arts, Smithsonian Institution

This lovely gray-haired girl was one of the light-colored Mandans. Catlin suspected that the Mandans were descended from a lost band of Welsh voyagers who, he thought, came up the Mississippi in the fourteenth century. It was a popular theory in Catlin's day, though it was without basis in fact.

∾∾∾∾∾∾∾*O-Kee-Pa*∾∾∾∾∾∾∾

CATLIN AND HIS HOST, JAMES KIPP, HAD JUST sat down to breakfast one morning when they were startled by a terrible sound from the village. Women were shrieking and screaming, and dogs were howling. The whole community was in an uproar.

"Now we have it!" cried Kipp, "the grand ceremony has commenced!"

Rushing to the center of the village with his sketchbook, Catlin looked back over his shoulder and saw approaching the village from the West a solitary figure whose naked body was painted with white clay. The closer he came the louder grew the shouting and wailing of the Indians. Men went for their

85

bows and arrows and put black paint on their faces as if going
off to war. For this was Nu-mohk-muck-a-nah, the First Man,
and his appearance in the village was the long-awaited signal
to begin the ceremony of O-Kee-Pa.

Nu-mohk-muck-a-nah was in reality Old Bear, the chief
medicine man of the village. Catlin knew it, and the whole village knew it, but in this disguise Old Bear was acting out a part
he had performed each July for years. The villagers knew their
parts, too, and played them to the hilt.

For a whole day everyone went through the traditional roles.
Nu-mohk-muck-a-nah went to each lodge and demanded from
each one a knife or spear. Then he chose four men to prepare
the medicine lodge—to sweep it and arrange the floor with
buffalo skulls and other sacred objects. Meanwhile, twelve men
appeared in the central clearing to begin the Bull Dance. Eight
were dressed as buffalo. Two wore black paint to represent "the
night," and two were painted red and white, to signify "the
day."

All day the dance went on, as the villagers watched, howling
and screaming, from the rooftops. Toward sundown, Nu-mohk-
muck-a-nah carried his collection of spears and knives into the
medicine lodge. As he did so, the terrible noise and clamor
subsided, and not a sound was heard anywhere in the village
until the morning of the second day.

The sun was barely up before the noise began again. Nu-
mohk-muck-a-nah appeared again, this time followed by several
young men of the village, daubed with paint and carrying their
shields and weapons. As Catlin watched them pass stony-faced
into the sacred lodge, he felt a pang of disappointment. He
would miss seeing the rest of the ritual.

But Old Bear the medicine man had come to admire and
respect the artist during his weeks among the Mandans, and
without being asked, he now accorded to Catlin the highest

honor the tribe could give. Silently he singled Catlin out of
the crowd and, taking his arm, guided him through the door to
a special seat prepared for him inside the lodge.

For two endless days Catlin sat, transfixed, as one after
another the leaders of the tribe offered up speeches and prayers
to the Great Spirit. The young men neither spoke, nor moved,
throughout the whole time, nor were they allowed food or water
or even sleep.

Outside, the dancing and screaming continued. On the fourth
day, the Bull Dance was performed sixteen times, and by mid-
day the screaming was so loud Catlin thought everyone had gone
mad. Just then, as the unbearable noise reached its highest pitch,
the "Evil Spirit" came running into the village.

He was painted coal black with white circles. His appearance
seemed to throw the Indians into still greater panic. The women
and children, screaming, finally drove him back to the plain outside the village from which he had come.

Now a hush fell over the settlement. Men, women and children fell to the ground, exhausted. Inside the medicine lodge,
dimly lit and full of the smoke of pipes, it was time for the secret
part of the ceremony to begin, to find out how brave the silent
young men would prove to be.

So far, it had all been play-acting. But now the young men
must play their parts in earnest.

In the gloom of the lodge it was hard to see, but Catlin wished
he could see even less. Only his passionate devotion to the truth
kept him from turning away in horror from the sights he saw
that afternoon.

One at a time of the young fellows, already emaciated with fasting,
and thirsting, and waking, for nearly four days and nights, advanced
from the side of the lodge, and placed himself on his hands and feet
. . . for the performance of the operation, where he submitted to the
cruelties in the following manner: An inch or more of the flesh on each

INTERIOR OF
THE MANDAN
MEDICINE LODGE, *1832*

During the first three days of the O-Kee-Pa ceremony, the Master of the Ceremonies (center) cried continuously to the Great Spirit, while the young men, neither eating nor drinking nor sleeping, awaited the day of torture.

shoulder, or each breast was taken up between the thumb and finger by the man who held the knife in his right hand; and the knife, which had been ground sharp on both edges, and then hacked and notched with the blade of another, to make it produce as much pain as possible, was forced through the flesh below the fingers, and being withdrawn, was followed with a splint or skewer, from the other, who held a bunch of such in his left hand, and was ready to force them through the wound. There were then two cords lowered down from the top of the lodge (by men who were placed on the lodge outside, for the purpose), which were fastened to these splints or skewers, and they instantly began to haul him up; he was thus raised until his body was suspended from the ground where he rested, until the knife and a splint were passed through the flesh or integuments in a similar manner on each arm below the shoulder (over the *brachialis externus*), below the elbow (over the *extensor carpi radialis*), on the thighs (over the *vastus externus*), and below the knees (over the *peroneus*). . . .

Several of them seeing me making sketches, beckoned me to look at their faces, which I watched through all this horrid operation, without being able to detect anything but the pleasantest smiles as they looked me in the eye, while I could hear the knife rip through the flesh, and feel enough of it myself, to start involuntary and uncontrollable tears over my cheeks.

As soon as all the youths were hanging helpless like this, the second stage of the torture began. A group of onlookers came out of the shadows and with long poles they poked and prodded the victims until they were turning around faster and faster. After ten or fifteen minutes of this agony, all the young men fainted. To Catlin's relief, the ropes were then cut and the nearly-lifeless bodies lowered gently to the ground. But it was not an act of mercy—merely a preparation for the third stage. One by one the youths revived. But instead of going home they staggered to another part of the lodge where the little fingers of their left hands were chopped off with a hatchet. Some even allowed their forefingers to be hacked off as well.

National Collection of Fine Arts, Smithsonian Institution

At the time Catlin passed near them, the Arikaras had "recently sworn death and destruction to every white man who comes in their way; and there is no doubt that they are ready to execute their threats." Wisely, the artist decided not to visit their village, but painted their chief at a Hidatsa village where he was visiting.

During the whole of the time of this cruel part of these most extraordinary afflictions, the chiefs and dignitaries of the tribe are looking on, to decide who are the hardiest and "stoutest hearted"—who can hang the longest by his flesh before he faints, and who will be soonest up, after he has been down; that they may know whom to appoint to lead a war party, or place at the most honourable and desperate post.

Half-dead, the young men were now led outside to the center of the village, and in front of the whole tribe, they were dragged by the wrists across the ground. This was called the "Last Race."

When it was all over, Catlin's sketchbook was bursting with pictures, and his notebook was filled to overflowing with the most detailed account possible. He knew that nothing but the most detached, scientific account would be accepted by the "cits." Catlin himself could hardly believe what he had seen with his own two eyes; it was going to be nearly impossible to get others to believe it.

The ceremony had lasted four days. At the end, everyone in the village was exhausted. Catlin, too, was wrung out, though he had only watched. He was devoted to these people and their native good manners and generosity. Even after the horrors of the O-Kee-Pa he still loved them. Yet he longed now for the carefree company of Ba'tiste and Bogard again and for the simple pleasure of steering his canoe down the Missouri toward home.

Before they could leave, though, Catlin spent a week painting a series of four careful pictures—one for each day of the ceremony. For the historical record it was absolutely essential to put down every detail of the O-Kee-Pa ceremony exactly as he had witnessed it. After the work was finished, Catlin took one last precaution: he obtained, in writing, a certificate of its authenticity. Many years later, he would treasure this simple document more than any other.

We the undersigned, hereby certify that we witnessed with Mr. Catlin, the four days' religious ceremony of the Mandans, and that he faithfully represented those scenes in his four paintings, to which this certificate is attached, as we saw them transacted, without addition or exaggeration.

> J. KIPP,
> Agent of Fur Company at
> Fort Clarke, Mandan Village.
>
> L. CRAWFORD.
> Clerk of do.
>
> ABRAHAM BOGARD,
> Mandan Village, *23d July, 1832*.

Catlin would miss Four Bears and James Kipp, and the luxury of the Mandans' steam baths and wonderful cooking, but nothing looked so good right now as another spell at the stern paddle. Kipp gave his departing guests fresh food, some precious coffee, and a piece of invaluable advice: "Keep clear of the Arikaras."

National Collection of Fine Arts, Smithsonian Institution

The Big Elk was second chief of the Omahas. His face was painted black for war, but the medal around his neck, a gift from the President, stood for peace.

❧Prairie Fire❧

HEY HAD MADE A LATE START AND WERE
still paddling after sundown when they spotted a column
of smoke rising from the shore. A quick look through his spy-
glass was enough to convince Catlin that it came from an Arikara campfire. A second, closer look confirmed his worst fears:
a war party was encamped here, and above the fire, those objects
hanging from poles to dry were *fresh scalps.*

Once the Arikara had been a friendly tribe, but they had been
exploited for years by the fur traders. Now, in the summer of
1832, they were beginning to rebel against the white man. Not
even George Catlin wanted to investigate this tribe, this summer. Gone was his usual eager curiosity; Catlin was too con-

95

cerned with guarding his collection. In the canoe were his paintings, his Indian costumes and artifacts. Most important, he was carrying his notes and pictures of the secret Mandan ceremony. Nothing must happen to them!

But having decided to avoid the Arikaras, Catlin was dismayed to find that the force of the river's current was rushing the canoe, uncontrollably, straight toward the shore where the Arikaras were celebrating their recent victory. No amount of paddling could bring the canoe out of the current. In moments they would be beached like helpless fish right in the laps of the enemy. Desperately, they grabbed armfuls of floating brush into the canoe, dived under the branches, and held their breath.

They could hear the voices of some women splashing in the water. The voices grew louder and louder. Suddenly, they heard someone sing out: "Chee-ne-see-nun, chee-ne-see-nun ke-mon-shoo, kee-ne-he-na, ha-way-tah? shee-sha, shee-sha. (How do you do, how do you do? Where are you going, old tree? Come here, come here.)."

Then: "Lah-kee-hoon! lah-kee-hoon! natch, catogh! (A canoe, a canoe! See the paddle!)."

Incredibly, it was the Arikaras who were the most frightened. In an instant, they had doused their fire and muzzled their dogs. The astonished travelers lost no time in making their escape.

They paddled hard all night. Every once in a while the moonlight played tricks on them, and some breeze in the underbrush or some innocent raccoon would send the blood pounding to their heads. But when the sun finally returned, they saw nothing for miles in either direction except smooth water and quiet sand. They had made it!

Just to be on the safe side, they kept moving as long as there was daylight. Finally, exhausted, they pulled in their paddles and let the canoe drift in toward the shore. After a delicious dinner—hot food had never tasted so good—the travelers spread out their buffalo robes for a good long sleep, their first in thirty-six hours.

But, though they had eluded the ruthless Arikaras, Catlin and his companions had a new enemy to contend with: the famous Missouri River mosquitoes, more bloodthirsty than even the Arikaras, or so it seemed that night. As a matter of fact, Catlin could still remember that night so vividly that he wrote about it nine years later: "The mosquitoes met us with ten thousand kicks and cuffs, and importunities, until we were choked and strangled into almost irrevocable despair and madness." Finally, the savage insects forced them into action.

Downriver they could hear rapids, so they clearly couldn't continue their journey; it would be too dangerous in the dark. The only place to go was *up*. Ba'tiste was already scrambling up the clay bluffs like a madman. "Try, try!" he called. "Ce n'est pas difficile, Monsieur Cataline." Ba'tiste had found a small level place halfway up the hill where he said they might escape the torment of the mosquitoes.

"We spread one of our robes," wrote Catlin, "and having ranged ourselves side by side upon it, and drawn the other one over us, we commenced, without further delay, upon the pleasurable forgetfulness of toil and dangers which had agitated for us the past day and night."

No sooner did Ba'tiste and Bogard fall asleep than it began to rain. It was going to be a long, long night.

It rained . . . and rained . . . and rained. The three travelers sat out the miserable hours huddled under a buffalo skin, dozing by turns, and longing for daylight. But it wasn't until the sun rose, that they realized just how dismal their situation actually was. Wrote Catlin:

Oh, all ye brickmakers, ye plasterers, and soft-soap manufacturers!

97

put all your imaginations in a ferment together, and see if ye can invent a scene like this! Here *was* a "fix" to be sure. The sun arose in splendour and in full, upon this everlasting and boundless scene of *"saft soap"* and grease, which admitted us not to move. The whole hill was constituted entirely of tough clay, and on each side and above us there was no possibility of escape; and one single step over the brink of the place where we had ascended, would inevitably have launched us into the river below, the distance of an hundred feet! Here, looking like hogs just risen from a mud puddle, or a buffalo bull in his wallow, we sat, (*and had to sit*), admiring the wide-spread and beautiful landscape that lay steeping and smoking before us, and our little boat, that looked like a nutshell beneath us, hanging at the shore; telling stories and filling up the while with nonsensical garrulity, until the sun's warming rays had licked up the mud, and its dried surface, about eleven o'clock, gave us foothold, when we cautiously, but safely descended to the bottom; and then, at the last jump, which brought his feet to *terra firma,* Ba'tiste exclaimed, "Well, we have cheatee de dam muskeet, ha!"

Whether it was the men who cheated the mosquitoes, or the other way around, it must have been hard to tell. Three more miserable, bedraggled travelers had surely never greeted a sunrise. Though they made light of their misery, Catlin knew only too well that there were still hundreds of miles to go to reach the simple comforts of St. Louis. And the hours of daylight became shorter every day. Their luck would have to change for the better, or they'd have a hard time making St. Louis before winter.

The first task was to bail the rain water out of the canoe and dry out the gear. As the men worked, Catlin studied his crude map. The hasty retreat from the Arikaras had delivered them to a point farther along than he had at first realized. In just a day or two their canoe would reach the mouth of the Teton River. This meant that they would soon arrive at Fort Pierre; it also meant that Catlin would have to watch his step. Two months

The Grand Pawnee warrior wore his "medicine" in the form of buffalo heads painted on his face and chest.

earlier, Catlin's visit had ended in tragedy. If relatives and tribesmen of the Sioux Indian, the Dog, were still in the neighborhood there would be no more painting for Catlin at Fort Pierre.

As soon as the last rain-soaked robe had dried out, the canoe was quickly packed, with the artist's paints and brushes safely out of sight. The three companions took up their paddles in callused hands, and headed south.

The heavy rain had swollen the river and the current carried the canoe along swiftly. As the hills and bluffs sped by, Catlin thought back to the last time he came to Fort Pierre, limping across the endless prairies on swollen feet. How long ago that seemed! How different he was today from the innocent, eager Easterner who had passed this way before! On the way upriver he had been George Catlin, a tourist with a sketchbook and letters of introduction from Governor Clark in his baggage. Returning, he was "Te-ho-pe-nee Wash-ee," renowned Medicine White Man, newspaper reporter, painter and historian of scores of Indian tribes, witness to the sacred Mandan ceremonies, skilled buffalo hunter, and friend to most of the great Indian chiefs and leaders northwest of St. Louis.

At Fort Pierre they hardly recognized him. His skin was as brown as any Indian's. His clothing now was more Indian than otherwise, for he had long ago worn out his city clothes. Even his conversation was different after months of struggling to communicate with Ba'tiste. But Catlin was still enough of an Easterner to remember the joys of good food, good wine and a good bed—which is exactly what Mr. Laidlaw gave him.

Another rainy spell kept Catlin and his companions at the busy fort several days. Wisely, Catlin avoided the Sioux encampment where, Laidlaw told him, the story of the Dog was still very fresh in everyone's memory. He did make some portraits of the tall Cheyennes, and used the rest of his time talking over old times with his good friend One Horn, and writing in his notebooks while the rain pattered on the roof.

Once the weather cleared, the canoe was on the river again. The shallow water was full of driftwood and the going was hard.

At night, the three slept on sand bars, safe from mosquitoes and grizzly bears. By day they feasted on ripe grapes and enjoyed many a meal of duck, goose, and antelope.

The artist was fascinated by the rugged landscape, and over and over he insisted on getting out of the canoe to explore and paint. Ba'tiste and Bogard said he must be getting soft in the head—here he was, a grown man, and educated, too. Yet he was forever rushing up one hill and sliding down the next. Patiently Catlin tried to make them see the beautiful scenery as he did. But they were not artists, and the more Catlin would chatter about colors and contours, the drowsier they would become. Catlin finally gave up. For days they traveled this way, with Ba'tiste and Bogard less and less interested in artistic matters the nearer they came to their destination, and Catlin demanding to stop at every bend in the river to collect rocks or wildflowers, or to make a sketch. Once they stopped to visit the grave of Sgt. Charles Floyd, who had accompanied Lewis and Clark on their historic expedition twenty-six years earlier. He had died just three months after the group started out from St. Louis, and his body had been buried high on a lonely hill overlooking the Missouri some twelve hundred miles above St. Louis.

After a summer spent among the native Indians, Catlin somehow felt a need to communicate with another white explorer like himself, so he sat a long time that day beside the cedar post that marked the young soldier's grave, absorbing the utter stillness and solitude of the spot. Except for Ba'tiste and Bogard napping on the shore below, he could see no trace of another human being in any direction, only the hundreds of rolling hills and the plains covered with tall grass now browning in the September sun. In the midst of this peace and stillness, Catlin's thoughts turned to the future. In the year 1804, when Lewis and Clark left St. Louis on their historic journey, only two hundred families crossed the river at St. Louis to make homes in the West. Vividly he could see a day when this grass would be ripped up by the plow and dotted with houses and cattle. Towns would be here one day, and then cities and the noise and the smoke of factories. With a shudder, Catlin rose, dropped a handful of now wilted wildflowers on the grave of Sgt. Floyd, and strode down the hill to waken Bogard and Ba'tiste.

The three paddled ahead, always on the lookout for the sunken roots and logs that could wreck the frail canoe in an instant. With the passing of each day, Ba'tiste and Bogard became more cheerful. It wouldn't be long, now, they said. Soon they would be celebrating in St. Louis.

One day they saw a white man's crude log house. The next day there were several. They were headed for civilization, no doubt about it. Catlin was in no hurry to end this trip, but even he was thrilled when on the west bank of the river, just above the Platte, they came abreast of Belle Vue, the home of Major Dougherty. To Catlin, Belle Vue was so much like his father's house in Pennsylvania that he could hardly believe his eyes. It was a *real* house surrounded with gardens and outbuildings. Inside, there were fine furnishings and, best of all, books. Catlin's friend was a man of learning who had been agent for the Pawnees for some years now. He had dealt firmly with them, but had always taken their side against the greedy demands of the fur traders. The Major was convinced that the fur trade must be ended, for it was destroying the Pawnees. As he and Catlin talked late in front of the fireplace, the artist was reminded of the long discussions back in Litchfield, when the law students talked of justice and equality under law. It had been a long, long time since Catlin had talked like this. He found himself pouring out his own passionate beliefs: that the white man's diseases, his greed, his guns, his whiskey and his ignorance would soon put an end to the Indians' noble way of life.

Dougherty went to his desk and pulled out a report he was writing to the Secretary of War. Catlin, scanning the draft, was struck with the forcefullness of the words.

"It is my decided opinion," wrote Dougherty,

that, so long as the Fur Traders and trappers are permitted to reside among the Indians, all efforts of the Government to better their condition will be fruitless. . . . While the agent is advising the Indians to give up the chase and settle themselves, with a view of agricultural pursuits, the Traders are urging them out in search of skins. . . . It is a curious and melancholy fact, that while the Central Government is using every means and expense to promote the advancement of those aboriginal people, it is at the same time suffering the Traders to oppose and defeat the very objects of their intentions.

Catlin would have been happy to stay on in this familiar-seeming house until there was no more to say—even if the snows fell and the river turned to ice. But Bogard and Ba'tiste had waited long enough for their celebration in St. Louis. There would be, he promised them, only one more stop.

And what a stop it was!

Nine miles down river from Dougherty's, the three bearded, dirty, hungry and ragged visitors were met at the shore by a smart group of mounted soldiers. Their brass buttons glittered. Their faces shone. Their boots gleamed.

Fort Leavenworth seemed, after all those months in the wilderness, like a great gleaming, bustling city. As the Army required, everything was done with precision, from the first bugle call at dawn to the melancholy call of taps at the end of the day.

National Collection of Fine Arts, Smithsonian Institution

Catlin thought this man, also called the Prophet, was "very distinguished, and one of the principal leading men of the Black Hawk party." Captured with Black Hawk and imprisoned with him at Jefferson Barracks near St. Louis, he was a much bolder warrior than Black Hawk himself.

In regular shifts the blue-clad guards fixed their bayonets and marched smartly out to their posts. Amidst the comings and goings of the sentries a constant stream of soldiers, officers and ladies flowed from house to house and shop to shop. Except for the frequent braying of the bugle and the sound of an occasional shouted command, it could have been Market Street in Philadelphia.

But, like the men who lived their lives in the isolated fur forts, the officers and men at Fort Leavenworth were lonely and bored. The officers' wives did all they could to keep their men happy and occupied; they held balls and dinner parties almost every week, and though their gowns were a bit out-of-date, they took great pains to look elegant and fashionable despite the heat. But nothing cheered these men more than a visit from strangers. They overwhelmed Catlin with invitations to dine, to dance, to ride, to hunt. It was all very flattering, and Catlin was delighted to accept. Before he knew it, he had booked up almost all his evenings—and many of his days—for the next several weeks. An orderly was assigned to take care of Catlin's every wish. A barber came around to his quarters to shave him and soothe his parched skin with hot, steaming towels.

There were large numbers of Indians camped nearby, and Catlin quickly had his easel set up and his paints mixed. He was working faster than ever now that he knew he would soon be home. Some of the paintings he did at Fort Leavenworth were barely more than sketches done rapidly in brown on a plain background. In a few weeks, back in St. Louis, he could finish them at his leisure.

He painted Iowas, Konzas, Pawnees, Omahas, Otos, Missouris, Delawares, Kickapoos, Potawatomies, and many others. His brushes moved with a new sureness as he chatted easily with the curious Indian audience that always surrounded him at his work. Though he was almost out of paint and canvas, he improvised with what he had, thinning his last remaining colors, and then thinning them again.

Once in a while, as he stood at his easel, Catlin noticed something strange about the air. It had a faintly bitter smell. Sometimes it even made his eyes water. The Indians told him there was fire on the prairies, and sure enough, he could see far in the distance a curl of black smoke rising out of the plains.

Catlin meant to have a closer look, for he had heard about the great fires that swept the plains at this time of year. They were said to be terrifying but also very beautiful. Here was a chance to add something different to his collection of paintings. So, with Ba'tiste, Bogard, Patrick Raymond (another friend), and an Indian guide named Red Thunder, Catlin rode out of the fort to enjoy a picnic and to see what was happening. Red Thunder begged them to go no closer to the little black cloud. "It is the season of fire," he said, "and I fear, from the smell of the wind, that the Spirit is awake!"

"Red Thunder seems sullen today," said Bogard. "He startles at every rush of the wind, and he scowls at the whole world that is about him."

Patrick Raymond spoke up. Catlin, who had a fine ear for dialect, later tried to capture the accents of his Irish brogue:

I know by the expression on your face, mon, you have never seen the world on fire yet, and therefore you know nothin' at all of a hurly burly of this kind—did ye? Did ye iver see the fire in high-grass, runnin' with a strong wind, about five mile and the half, and thin hear it strike into a slash of dry cane brake!! I would jist ax you that!! By thunder you niver have—for your eyes would jist stick out of your head at the thought of it. . . . Ask Jack Sanford, he's a chop that can tell you all aboot it. . . . If I were advisin', I would say that we are gettin too far into this imbustible meadow; for the grass is dry, and the wind is too strong to make a light matter of at this sason of he year. . . . Hello, what's that?

In a flash Red Thunder had charged off through the high grass towards home. The grass was so high that he disappeared in an instant, leaving the rest to dash after him blindly. The wind was pounding at their backs as they fled. An eagle swept over their heads screaming. Still the winds increased and they could hear a mighty roar growing louder behind them. But there was no looking back now. The men rode for their lives, but still antelopes overtook them and heath hens and rabbits shot by as if the riders were standing still. Dimly Catlin was aware of thunder, and in a flash of lightning he could see Red Thunder's horse leaping up the sides of a bluff ahead. The terrified horses needed no urging. Foaming, the other horses rushed to follow Red Thunder. At last they were safe above the sea of fire below. When they turned to look back from where they had come, they could see nothing but crimson fire from one end of the plain to the other. They had seen the great Fire Spirit, and the Fire Spirit had spared them!

One last time, Catlin, Ba'tiste and Bogard loaded the canoe, and one last time they said goodby to good friends. There had been too many farewells, thought Catlin sadly: One Horn, Four Bears, Major Sanford, Major Dougherty, the Crows, the Blackfeet, the Assiniboins—he would miss them all. Each time he said goodby, he promised to come back and see his friends, and each time he wondered in his heart if he ever would pass this way again.

They entered the Lower Missouri now, big, wide and muddy. They saw no more geese and ducks, for the fall migrations were over. Instead of the fields of butterfly weed there were only dry stalks, spiky with brown seedpods. The grass had long ago lost its greenness. At night, the heavens were filled with winter constellations, and the three huddled closer to the fire under their buffalo robes, feet to the fire Indian style.

PRAIRIE
FIRE, *1832*

When, at last, they swung out of the Missouri into the Mississippi, they cheered like boys. Twenty miles to go! Though they had steered the little boat two thousand miles, those last twenty seemed by far the longest. The six-mile-an-hour Missouri current that had speeded the canoe this far, was swallowed up by the slow Mississippi. The money in Ba'tiste and Bogard's pockets fairly burned to be spent in the big city. The celebration they had talked of so often was so close now that they could almost taste it. Catlin was eager, too, in his own way. He couldn't wait to unpack all his Indian treasures and to spread out his paintings in his hotel room. How many were there? Two hundred? Three? Some had come down river ahead of him on the *Yellowstone*; others he had entrusted to passing travelers and ship captains. What if any of them were lost? It was a thought too awful to consider.

They berthed the little canoe between two huge steamers at the St. Louis waterfront. Gruffly, the three embraced each other, and then Ba'tiste and Bogard did a little jig on the dock. With a joke and a whoop, they were off, racing toward the best saloon in town. Catlin shouldered his few belongings and headed for his hotel.

Waiting for him were almost all of the parcels he had sent on ahead. But when he returned later for his canoe, it was gone. In two thousand miles of traveling among the "savages," no one had ever laid a hand on it, but here in the "civilized world" it was stolen in a matter of hours. So much, thought Catlin, for the white man's famous honesty!

The newspapers were full of bad news. President Andrew Jackson's policy toward Catlin's new friends was being openly referred to as "Indian Removal," and it was being carried out with deadly seriousness. Even as Catlin was racing against the clock to record the faces and pastimes of the Northern Plains Indians, the Indians of the Deep South were signing documents they could not read, turning their hunting and farming lands over to the white man for pennies an acre. And while Catlin was watching the slaughter of the buffalo at Fort Union, Black Hawk, gallant chief of the Sauk and Foxes, was rallying his men in a last desperate attempt to stop white occupation of Illinois.

On August 3, 1832, Black Hawk was driven by soldiers to the banks of the Mississippi, where he surrendered.

"You have taken me a prisoner, with all my warriors," cried Black Hawk.

When I saw that I could not beat you, by Indian fighting, I determined to rush on you, and fight you face to face. I fought hard—but your guns were well aimed; the bullets flew like birds in the air, and whizzed by our ears, like the wind through the trees in the winter. My warriors fell around me—it began to look dismal. I saw my evil day at hand. The sun rose dim on us in the morning, and at night it sunk in a dark cloud, and looked like a ball of fire. That was the Last Sun, that shone on Black Hawk. His heart is dead, and no longer beats quick in his bosom. He is now a prisoner to the white men—they will do with him as they wish; but he can stand Torture, and is not afraid of Death! He is no coward. Black Hawk is an Indian.

He has done nothing, for which an Indian ought to be ashamed. He has fought for his countrymen, the squaws, and papooses, against white men, who came year after year, to cheat them, and take away their lands. He is satisfied; he will go to the land of spirits contented; he has done his duty; his father will meet him there, and commend him.

Black Hawk is a true Indian, and disdains to cry, like a woman. He feels for his wife, his children, and his friends—but he does not care for himself. Farewell, my Nation!——Black Hawk tried to save you, and avenge your wrongs. He drank the blood of some of the whites. He has been taken prisoner, and his plans are stopped; he can do no more: He is near end; his sun is setting, and will rise no more! FARE-WELL TO BLACK HAWK!!!

They brought him to St. Louis in chains, and when Catlin went to paint his portrait in Jefferson Barracks, Black Hawk was dressed only in simple buckskin. But the chief endured his imprisonment with great dignity. When he was taken to Washington City to talk with President Jackson, he said, simply, "You are a man; I am another."

The Mississippi was soon frozen, and his old chest pains returned, so Catlin loaded up a mule and set off for Florida in search of sunshine.

His brother, James, welcomed him in Pensacola where vermillion flowers bloomed the year round, the fruits burst with sweetness, and the Gulf Stream warmed the wide, lonely beaches. He explored the countryside around Pensacola in search of Indians, but found only a few, and, like all Indians who lived close to white men, he found them "pitiable."

Catlin was fond of his brother, but there was a difference of several years between them, and after a while the artist and the clerk ran out of things to talk about. Restlessness again took over, and the minute he could, he headed back to work on his precious paintings.

When spring came and river travel opened up again, he took a portion of his collection up the Ohio River, showing his paintings in Cincinnati and other towns along the way.

Clara was with him now, at long last; they were in Cincinnati from May to November. Catlin still had work to do on the paintings he brought back, some still only half-finished, from his trip the year before. Luckily, Governor Clark's nephew, Major Benjamin O'Fallon, ordered a set of Indian portraits for his country home near St. Louis, and though it meant copying his work all over again, Catlin was glad of the money, for Cincinnati was still only an isolated village, and goods were expensive. The set was finished by September. In October, Catlin held another exhibition of Indian portraits, and the proceeds, together with Major O'Fallon's generous payment, added up to a tidy sum. By Christmas George and Clara were in Louisville and in January they went to Pensacola.

How good it had been to have Clara by his side this past year! She always kept his spirits up. He hadn't really minded the tedium of making copies of his own pictures, as long as Clara was there.

Yet that winter George spent more and more time alone, pacing the beach, and pondering the future. It would only take another few months to perfect the canvases he already had. There were more than two hundred in the collection, and they represented twenty-seven different Indian tribes. He could soon have his collection in New York for a full-scale public showing.

New York, he knew, was already impatient to see the Indian Collection. His reports in the *Commercial Advertiser* newspaper had set the stage already; in them, the "cits" had been reading about the Great Plains, the buffalo, the ceremonies, the costumes, and the philosophy of the Indians. Now they waited eagerly to *see* it all with their own eyes.

And he could be with lovely Clara, always, and could begin to share with her the admiration and applause he was sure awaited him in the East. He knew this would please Clara more than anything he could do.

But once he left the frontier, and settled down among the "cits," could he ever come back to finish the job he had set out to do? In a year or two, or ten, would there be anything left to paint? Almost daily the condition of the Indians west of the Mississippi was worsening. Band after band, tribe after tribe, they were being hustled and herded further west. At the same time, the Mexicans, desperate to hold on to their claim to the Southwest, were pushing up into Texas. Besides, armies of missionaries were fanning out across the prairies, bent on erasing

National Collection of Fine Arts, Smithsonian Institution

This Sauk and Fox warrior, another of the prisoners at Jefferson Barracks, told Catlin that his spear had killed four white men during the Black Hawk War.

the Indians' "savage" beliefs and traditions. Some of the missionaries had already pushed all the way to Oregon. Meanwhile, bigger and better steamboats were carrying more and more cheap trade goods and whiskey and smallpox to the remote villages where Indians had been safe before to lead their own lives. And each summer, there was just a little less game. Surely, Indian life could not go on much longer in the old way.

Clara and George had never had a home of their own—what little time they had together was spent in boardinghouses or with relatives. She longed to be a real, year-round wife, with a real house and real children.

So when George told her that her dreams would have to wait just a little longer, she must have been bitterly disappointed. George promised that after one last trip, he'd never go away from her again. He *must* visit the tribes of the Southwest before his work was complete. There would only be one more goodby. That was a promise.

National Collection of Fine Arts, Smithsonian Institution

This man was the champion ball-player of the Choctaw nation. The game was played like a sort of aerial hockey, with no one allowed to touch the ball except with the two racquets.

~~~~Comanche Country~~~~

THE OMENS WERE NOT GOOD. ALMOST FROM the moment Clara's steamer disappeared around the bend, things began to go wrong. At first they were just little things, but Catlin soon began to feel a sense of foreboding that was to haunt him for many months.

Through friends, Catlin had obtained the approval of Lewis Cass, the Secretary of War, to venture into the treacherous, un-mapped regions of the Southwest. This was the land of the dreaded Comanche; the land of deserts and searing heat and rattlesnakes. For his own safety, he would have to travel with the Army, for no one could survive alone without quantities of food, water and ammunition. It happened that such an expedition was

117

being readied at Fort Gibson. As soon as he had Secretary Cass's letter in hand, and his paints mixed, the artist was eager to be off.

But first, he had to travel up the Arkansas River by steamer some seven hundred miles to Fort Gibson to join the expedition. It was here that the first piece of bad luck occurred: the river was low, much too low even for a small boat like the *Arkansas*. Time after time, they ran aground. Once the ship lay helpless on a sand bar for more than two weeks, waiting for rains that didn't come. The passengers passed the time on land hunting and fishing, or playing cards. Finally they began catching centipedes and tarantulas, laying bets as to which could kill the other first.

Catlin was sure that the long delay would cause him to miss his chance. Surely by now the regiment would have started.

But when the *Arkansas* finally arrived at Fort Gibson, things were still far from ready for a departure. Many of the troops had not yet arrived. Provisions were still to be procured and distributed. The atmosphere at the fort was one of confusion and uncertainty, and Catlin's feeling of uneasiness grew a bit stronger. Besides, everything at Fort Gibson reminded George of Julius. His brother seemed to haunt the plains and the very air around the fort. The sky, the river, the wildlife were all just as Julius had described them in his letters. Eight years had passed since Julius took his last walk along the Arkansas River after resigning his commission. But bitter thoughts rushed back to George—thoughts he had tried to bury long ago: if it hadn't been for him, Julius might be here today. He would be a Captain or a Major now, and they would make this journey side by side, riding, sleeping, eating together, talking over old times.

If only the regiment would get organized and leave this place! The days dragged on and on. Nobody seemed to have any idea when the journey would start. Catlin, hounded by his painful memories, spent the time among the thousands of Indians living or camping nearby. The stories they had to tell only gave the artist more to brood about, for many of them were Cherokees, Creeks and Seminoles. Having been forced off their ancestral lands in Alabama, Florida and Georgia, and having made the long journey, many of them on foot, through all kinds of weather, they were now trying pathetically to farm this new land of theirs. They were unused to the long droughts and harsh winters of the Oklahoma plains, and their homesickness was painful to see. Their unhappiness only added to Catlin's gloom. He tried to shake it off by riding far out to the southwest, where he found large numbers of Osages still living in their traditional ways, shaving their heads, all but a scalplock, and dressing in well-made robes.

Besides the Osages, Catlin met and painted the Choctaws, who, he found to his delight, were first-rate horsemen and athletes. He spent hour after hour sketching their ball games and feats of horsemanship. Here among the Choctaws, Catlin felt almost carefree. These were a joyous people. Although they had been banished from their southern homelands, they were making a success of their new life. Their farms prospered, they abstained from whiskey, and somehow they had held onto their sense of humor.

Among the Choctaws, painting and joking, Catlin lost all sense of time. But at Fort Gibson the complex preparations for the long trip were finally coming to an end, and word was sent to Catlin that the time for departure had arrived. It was the middle of June now. The expedition should have left two months earlier—even the leaders of the regiment admitted as much. Now, instead of pleasant weather, they would start out under a blazing sun, and they would be returning in the path of hailstorms and tornadoes.

Catlin was hardened to outdoor life; he had no fear of storms or droughts. What disturbed him was the First Dragoon regiment itself. Now that the troops were all assembled, Catlin

Thomas Gilcrease Institute

could see that they made a full-scale military force. They passed in review, four-hundred-fifty strong, each company mounted on splendid horses of a uniform color, armed with the latest and most efficient firearms, dressed not for the parade ground, but for the battlefield.

The purpose of the expedition was to meet peacefully with the supposedly wild tribes of the Southwest, and to make friends. But what, wondered Catlin, would the Indians think when their scouts beheld this mile-long column of armed cavalry? Surely they would flee for their lives. "We are invaders of a sacred soil," Catlin mused. "We are carrying war in our front."

On June 19, 1834, to the sound of bugles blowing and leather boots creaking against saddles, the regiment streamed out through the gates of Fort Gibson. General Henry Leavenworth rode at the head of the column and Catlin, who was assigned to his staff, followed close behind. Minutes before, Catlin had handed someone a letter to be sent to his brother-in-law. "I start this morning with the dragoons for Pawnee country," it said, "but God only knows where that is."

It was a fine looking regiment and General Leavenworth was in a good mood, pleased to be starting at last. He set a brisk pace of march across the plains, and the horses and men and baggage

White Weasel, a Kiowa girl, and her little brother, the Thunder, had been for many years prisoners of the Osage when Catlin met them. Before the Dragoons set out from Ft. Gibson, Col. Dodge bought them back from their captors. As a gesture of government friendship, the children were brought back to their native village, where they were reunited with their relatives. Catlin was at his best in some of his quick water color sketches. Here he captured the whole story of the girl's life in one small, pensive picture.

121

wagons and Indian guides and pack horses followed with a will.

When they came to a river, they swam it, and when they came to a ridge, they crossed it with hardly a break in the ranks or a slowing of the steady, disciplined pace.

With every mile they traveled, Catlin's admiration for his new horse, Charley, grew deeper. Back at Fort Gibson, where he had bought Charley, they had told him this was "the finest horse known in that section of the country," and now Catlin could see why. Charley was high-spirited and handsome, cream colored with a fine long black mane and tail. He proved to be tireless on the long trail, never faltering no matter what was asked of him. And when the column halted to rest, Charley still had so much "gumption" that Catlin would have to take him for a good gallop. Catlin had paid $250.00 for Charley— a huge price for that time and place—but he never had cause to regret it.

The first few days went beautifully; there was plenty to eat on the supply wagons, and wild plums and berries fairly choked the prairie grass. Buffalo were so abundant that General Leavenworth or Colonel Dodge frequently called a halt to give the men a chance for a little shooting.

Then one morning the order to move out was late in sounding. Some of the soldiers had taken sick during the night, and a number of the horses appeared to be sick, too. On the twentieth day the bugle did not blow at all. Now nearly half the men were seriously ill, and it was decided to lay over a few days on the Red River at the mouth of the Washita. The regimental surgeon feared that many of the men might die if the march continued.

Days passed on the riverbank overlooking Texas, but instead of recuperating, the men grew worse. They fainted and vomited. Their skins and even their eyeballs turned yellow. They writhed on their blankets, lost in delirium. General Leavenworth himself lay groaning in his tent, near death. There was only one thing to do: the party would be divided in half, with those well enough to travel going forward under the command of Colonel Henry Dodge; the sick would stay at the encampment.

If Catlin had any symptoms of the disease, he told no one. He *must* be with the group when they made contact with the Comanches. After all the traveling and all the months of waiting, to end the journey now was unthinkable.

So Colonel Dodge moved out with two hundred men, and Catlin was among them. Much of the remaining food and nearly all the water had to be left behind for the sick; Colonel Dodge's party would have to shift for themselves.

Each day more soldiers came down with the fever, but they plodded on and on, seeing occasionally a swirl of smoke from an Indian fire far in the distance. They were well into Comanche country now. They knew the Comanches were watching them. When would they show themselves?

Riding along on Charley's broad back, Catlin, too, was beginning to feel strange. Though he searched the horizon constantly for a glimpse of the Indians, he felt his vision dimming. Lord, it was hot! He took to carrying an umbrella in the hope of fending off the crushing heat.

On the fourth day, at noon, a large group of horsemen was spotted, watching. They were several miles away, and it looked at first as if they might be Mexican cavalry, which would have meant trouble. But a closer look revealed them to be Comanche warriors. Colonel Dodge and his men started toward them, but they disappeared from their hilltop, later reappearing farther away. The maneuver was repeated several times until Colonel Dodge, realizing the Indians might be frightened, rode out with only a few men. This time, the Indians stood their ground. Then one of the Indians, carrying a white flag, began to gallop toward the strangers. Later, they learned his name: the Little Spaniard.

DRAGOONS
APPROACHING
COMANCHE VILLAGE
1834

After their first nervous encounter with the U. S. Army, the Comanches ordered their horses to line up just as smartly as Col. Dodge had lined up his Dragoons.

Catlin wrote:

The distance between the two parties was perhaps half a mile, and that a beautiful and gently sloping prairie over which he was for the space of a quarter of an hour, reining and spurring his maddened horse, and gradually approaching us by tacking to the right and the left, like a vessel beating against the wind. He at length came prancing and leaping along until he met the flag of the regiment, when he leaned his spear for a moment against it, looking the bearer full in the face, then he wheeled his horse, and dashed up to Colonel Dodge with his extended hand, which was instantly grasped and shaken. We all had him by the hand in a moment, and the rest of the party seeing him received in this friendly manner, instead of being sacrificed, as they undoubtedly expected, started under "full whip" in a direct line towards us, and in a moment gathered, like a black cloud, around us! The regiment then moved up in regular order, and a general shake of the hand ensued, which was accomplished by each warrior riding along the ranks, and shaking the hand of every one as he passed.

The peace pipe was handed around, and the leaders made speeches of friendship. When the Comanches heard about the strange and violent illness they offered to lead the way west. It was rough, rocky country ahead, and the going was slow. Though Catlin could feel the strength leaving his body, he fought off the disease as long as he could. When at last they reached the Comanche settlement, he was still able to marvel at the herds of wild horses. And he was still keeping a journal:

The Camanchees [sic] are in stature, rather low, and in person, often approaching to corpulency. In their movements, they are heavy and ungraceful; and on their feet, one of the most unattractive and slovenly-looking races of Indians that I have ever seen; but the moment they mount their horses, they seem at once metamorphosed, and surprise the spectator with the ease and elegance of their movements. A Camanchee on his feet is out of his element, and comparatively almost as awkward as a monkey on the ground, without a limb or a branch to cling to! but the moment he lays his hand upon his horse, his *face,* even, becomes handsome, and he gracefully flies away like a different being.

At last, Catlin had to give up the struggle. He had a burning fever and ached with chills and nausea. Colonel Dodge was going to push onward to meet the Wichitas. He could take only the healthy ones; the rest must await his return here at the Comanche village. Catlin was so sick that he hardly noticed their departure. Later, he heard about their friendly encounter with the Wichitas: Colonel Dodge was able to convince them that the American government was their friend. The Indians, seeing the pitiable condition of the soldiers, offered to guide them back to Fort Gibson.

Catlin, more dead than alive, was gently lifted onto a litter slung between two horses. Beside him rode his faithful friend, Joe Chadwick. The next two weeks were nightmarish for everyone. The whole countryside was parched with such a drought as had never been known before. The sun burned down on them without mercy. Soon there was no more fresh water to drink, so they plunged their canteens into the foul, stagnant water of the buffalo wallows. They watched numbly while their horses, drinking from the same pools, fell dead in their tracks. But they drank the water anyway. Off in the distance they sometimes saw—or thought they saw—rain clouds dumping sweet fresh showers on some far-off prairie, out of reach, a day's ride or more away. Meanwhile, horses and men kept dying. Many of them had to be left beside the trail to make it as best they could.

Every once in a while Catlin would see some unusual mineral or fossil on the ground below his litter. Agreeably, Joe Chadwick would pick it up and hand it to his friend. But eventually the rock collection grew too heavy, and Chadwick had to empty the sack onto the ground.

Catlin became delirious and could no longer ride the litter, so

National Collection of Fine Arts, Smithsonian Institution

This Comanche chief led Col. Dodge's party on to the Comanche village, where they could rest. He was dressed for a war party when the Dragoons were sighted, but he and the other warriors postponed their feud to help the stricken soldiers. Col. Dodge later gave him a fine rifle for his services.

they laid him in an empty baggage wagon, where he jounced and jiggled helplessly for days as the wagon creaked across the sun-baked, rock-hard trail.

One day, Catlin opened his eyes to find a man studying him intently. It was a familiar face, but before he could place it, he slid back into unconsciousness. The next time he woke, he saw that he was in a cool, shadowy room back at Fort Gibson. He could not move, or speak, but the familiar face came back and Catlin managed a smile, for this was his old schoolmate from Wilkes-Barre, Joseph Jefferson Burr Wright, now a doctor assigned to the frontier. By some miracle, Dr. Wright had pulled him through, and Catlin struggled to express his gratitude. But the words didn't come. Soundlessly Catlin began to weep. Dr. Wright adjusted his pillow and crept out of the room.

Very gradually, Catlin's strength came back, but the awful depression stayed with him, a result of his illness that he hated worse than the pain or the fever.

A graveyard had been created outside Catlin's window, and while he lay miserably in his bed, muffled drums beat endlessly as the dead were carried out to their final resting place. These wretched funerals—sometimes six or eight of them a day—drifted in and out of Catlin's nightmares. The coffins sometimes seemed to be Julius's, sometimes his own, and he would wake up with tears in his eyes.

As his mind slowly cleared, Catlin became convinced that he would never recover fully at Fort Gibson, among the gruesome sights and sounds and smells. With every shred of will power he could muster, he fought off the lingering illness. It took many weeks, but at last, he was able to get up and walk around a little bit.

Dr. Wright told him he was too weak to travel; he'd never get ten miles, but Catlin knew he had to try. So Charley was saddled up one morning, and Joe Chadwick helped his friend up.

WOLVES WATCH
FROM A DISTANCE
AS CATLIN AND CHARLEY
SETTLE DOWN
FOR THE NIGHT, *1841*

From an illustration in
Catlin's book, *Letters and
Notes on the Manners, Customs, and Condition of the
North American Indians.*

All alone, Charley and his master set off across the plains, leaving behind them the smell of death and the fear of dying. Far ahead lay the cool Missouri Valley, five hundred miles to the north, and beyond that, thank God, Clara was waiting for him.

Charley, sensing Catlin's condition, stepped carefully through the grasses and across the dry gullies, following almost instinctively the arrow on his master's pocket compass. Under the open sky, Catlin grew better and stronger each day. He was almost sure now that he had escaped the grave, though he still had chills so violent that he had to dismount and lie on the ground until they passed. The awful urge to weep was going away, too. And when he threw his line into a stream and brought in his first fish, he grinned a great grin. By golly, he and Charley were going to make it!

Soon, he was able to organize his thoughts enough to write in his journal again. Sitting by the campfire, he thought over the events of the disastrous summer, and wondered if any good would come of it.

As far as it went, the expedition had been a success for the government. Colonel Dodge had brought together under a genuine flag of truce the head chiefs of the Wichita, Comanche, Kiowa and Waco tribes. They had held a very friendly council, passed the pipe, and parted on the best of terms. And from Catlin's point of view, it had to be counted as a small triumph. He had come away with his life, and with his notebooks and paintings intact.

But the cost had been enormous. General Leavenworth dead, along with nearly two hundred officers and men—and more were still dying every day.

"Although the achievement has been a handsome one," the artist wrote,

of bringing these unknown people to an acquaintance, and a general peace; and at first sight would appear to be of great benefit to them—yet I have my strong doubts, whether it will better their condition, unless with the exercised aid of the strong arm of the Government, they can be protected in the rights which, by nature, they are entitled to.

There is already in this place a company of eighty men fitted out, who are to start to-morrow, to overtake these Indians a few miles from this place, and accompany them home, with a large stock of goods, with traps for catching beavers, &c., calculating to build a trading-house amongst them, where they will amass, at once, an immense fortune, being the first traders and trappers that have ever been in that part of the country.

So, there they were again, the fur traders, ready to move in the minute the government had met the Indians and found them friendly. Catlin had seen the pattern too often before, and he knew it spelled the doom of still more tribes.

~~~~~*Pipes of Peace*~~~~~

*I*T WAS NEARLY MIDNIGHT IN ALTON, ILLI-
nois, when Clara Catlin was awakened by faint sounds at the
front door. She slipped on a warm wrapper and groped her way
down the cold hallway, a candlestick in her hand. Through the
window she saw leaning against the door a bearded stranger
with a sunken face and hollow eyes. His clothes hung in rags
from his bony shoulders. A beggar? At this hour? The candle
brightened for a moment and Clara saw, with horror, that this
was her George.

She flung the door open and caught the apparition just as he
started to fall. Pulling him into the parlor, she laid him in front
of the fire, brought him a hot drink, put his head on her lap

134

and waited for him to speak. He whispered his story in short, disjointed sentences at first, but as she stroked his forehead he began to speak more steadily. He told her about the waiting, the fevers, the deaths, the drought, the blazing sun, the poisoned water. Sometimes he spoke of Julius, too. When he finished his garbled tale, the sun was already up. Gently Clara led him to bed and tucked him in.

For a long time, Catlin seemed content to follow Clara everywhere. At night he was plagued with terrible dreams, and only she could soothe him back to sleep. His exhausted body needed the care that only Clara could give. Nothing else seemed to matter to him. When his latest paintings arrived on the steamer, he showed no interest in them.

Clara had never seen her husband like this. It worried her deeply that he was so changed. As soon as he could travel, she persuaded him to go south. A fresh scene and a sunny climate would do him good. It always had before.

But after passing the winter on the Gulf of Mexico, he still looked pale and tired. If only he would take up his work again! Clara knew that he wasn't ready to go anywhere alone, so she laid a subtle campaign of her own: Why not spend the summer just being tourists, she suggested. They would book a stateroom on one of the "floating palaces" heading up the Mississippi from New Orleans to Fort Snelling, where St. Paul stands today.

Clara convinced George that she wanted this trip more than anything. So, to please Clara, he agreed. While they were packing, Clara remarked casually that he might as well bring the paints and canvas along, just in case. . . .

Though this was to be "Clara's trip," George himself began to perk up a bit as the big side-wheeler swept along on the broad river. They had decided to make a long stopover at Fort Snelling, and Catlin seemed to be gaining enthusiasm as each day brought them closer to their destination.

Finally, they could see the fort in the distance, its battlements dominating the entire countryside from the top of a bluff. Below, at the water's edge, Indian lodges stood clustered together by the dozens.

Clara's eyes shone with excitement at seeing her first Indian encampment. She begged George to take her there, and soon they were mingling with the Sioux, who were settled on the west bank of the Mississippi, and the Chippewas, who were staying on the opposite bank. The Chippewa women made a great fuss over Clara, clamoring to shake her hand. They showed off their babies to her, and charmed her with gifts of maple sugar candy. Before long they were inviting her into their lodges.

Clara loved Fort Snelling. Every week elegant river boats arrived from St. Louis, loaded with tourists and fashionable visitors, so there were always new friends to meet and new people to talk to. In the officers' quarters, where the Catlins stayed, there were polite orderlies to wait on them, and they soon felt pleasantly pampered.

And George began to paint again. The elaborate cradles of the Chippewas were more than he could resist; he sketched these, and then went on to portraits and landscapes. The holiday was doing George a world of good, thought Clara, as she watched him talking and laughing with the Indians. She knew the cure was complete when, at the end of the summer, he announced that he would go home by canoe. There were many tribes between here and St. Louis. He couldn't possibly paint them from the deck of a steamer.

Late in August, Catlin put his wife on a southbound boat and stood on the little landing below the fort as it churned out of sight, missing her already.

Clara was to travel ahead of him in stages. He was to paddle his canoe as fast as he could, and catch up with her in Prairie du Chien, and then later they would separate and meet again further downriver. It would be like a game of hide and seek. If only he could look forward to meeting Clara this way on all his journeys!

In a happy frame of mind, George followed his wife down the Mississippi, his canoe nudged by the steady current. He dined on bass and duck and plums, and filled his pockets with agates, carnelians, jaspers and porphyry, and fell asleep to the call of the whippoorwill. He marveled at the great migrating flocks which overtook his slow little craft on their way south, and admired the fast-changing colors of autumn.

He arrived at Prairie du Chien on schedule and Clara was there to greet him. After a few weeks with the Menominees and Winnebagos, they parted and met again at Dubuque. Then for a time they traveled together on a steamer, Catlin's little canoe riding on the deck.

Finally, at Camp des Moines, the little game had to end, for winter was on the way, and Clara must hurry back to the safety and comfort of St. Louis. Before she left, Catlin tucked her and two friends into his canoe and paddled them skillfully through the Des Moines rapids. Soaked with spray, but glowing with excitement, Clara boarded the steamer at the foot of the rapids. George thought she had never looked so beautiful.

In a week or so, Catlin was settled beside his own fireplace in St. Louis, with Clara and Joe Chadwick. Joe, who had stuck by Catlin so faithfully through the previous summer, was sitting for his portrait, and listening with Clara as George told them how he came to arrive home without his treasured pistols.

During the part of the journey he and Clara had passed together on the steamer, Catlin had seen from the deck a stretch of country he wanted to explore, so, after saying goodby to her, he had paddled out onto the river to wait for a northbound boat to take him there.

137

During his vacation with Clara on the Mississippi, Catlin painted this stoic Chippewa mother near Ft. Snelling.

I at length discovered a steamer several miles below me, advancing through the rapids, and in the interim I set to and cleaned my fowling-piece and a noble pair of pistols, which I had carried in a belt at my side, through my buffalo and other sports of the west, and having put them in fine order and deposited them in the bottom of the canoe before me, and taken my paddle in hand, with which my long practice had given me unlimited confidence, I put off to the middle of the river, which was there a mile and a half in width, to meet the steamer. . . . I made my signal as I neared the steamer, and desired my old friend, Captain Rogers, not to stop his engine; feeling full confidence that I could, with an *Indian touch* of the paddle, toss my little bark around, and gently grapple to the side of the steamer, which was loaded down, with her gunnels near to the water's edge. Oh, that my skill had been equal to my imagination, or that I could have had at that moment the balance and skill of an Indian *woman,* for the sake of my little craft and what was in it!

Before he could get a good grip, someone threw a rope from the deck, which accidentally snared the front of the canoe. The canoe tipped over, sending his guns to the bottom, and throwing the artist into the rolling current.

If I had drowned, my death would have been witnessed by at least an hundred ladies and gentlemen who were looking on, but I *did not.* —I soon took a peep, by the side of my trunk etc., above the water, and for the first time in my life was "collared," and that by my friend Captain Rogers, who undoubtedly saved me from making further explorations on the river bottom, by pulling me into the boat, to the amusement of all on deck, many of whom were my old acquaintances, and not knowing the preliminaries, were as much astounded at my sudden appearance, as if I had been disgorged from a whale's belly. A small boat was sent off for my trunk, which was picked up about half a mile below and brought on board full of water, and, consequently, clothes, and sketchbooks and everything else entirely wet through. My canoe was brought on board, which was several degrees dearer to me now than it had been for its long and faithful service; but my gun and pistols are there yet.

. . . I remained on board for several miles, till we were passing a wild and romantic rocky shore, on which the sun was shining warm, and I launched my little boat into the water, with my trunk in it and put off to the shore, where I soon had every paper and a hundred other things spread in the sun, and at night in good order for my camp, which was at the mouth of a quiet little brook, where I caught some fine bass and fared well, till a couple of hours paddling the next morning brought me back to Camp Des Moines.

"Egad!" said Joe. "How I should like to have been with you!"
"Sit still, or I shall lose your likeness."

Catlin's tale went on, and though Joe was itching to laugh he held his pose. Once his things were dry, Catlin had proceeded upriver ninety miles to Rock Island. Starting toward home one fine day, he stopped to rest in the afternoon, drawing the canoe onto the beach as usual. Paddle in hand, he strolled up the bank to have a look around, "to see what might be seen; when, in a minute or two, I turned towards the river, and, to my almost annihilating surprise and vexation, I saw my little canoe some twenty or thirty rods from the shore, and some distance below me, with its head aiming across the river, and steadily gliding along in that direction, where the wind was roguishly wafting it!"

He ran down the beach, flinging off his clothes as he went, and dived naked into the chilly water in pursuit. But he was no match for the wind and the current. The saucy little canoe had escaped. Returning to shore, the disgusted painter collected his clothes and set about to rescue himself. "I am here on a desolate island," he thought, "with nothing to eat, and destitute of the means of procuring anything; and if I pass the night, or half a dozen of them here, I shall have neither fire nor clothes to make me comfortable; and nothing short of *having my canoe* will answer me at all."

So Catlin built a clumsy raft out of half-rotten driftwood and set sail in the direction of his canoe, across the mile-wide river.

The raft got him across the river, but only barely, for in the end he was riding waist-deep in the water. When he reached the shore, the raft fell apart completely. Fortunately he found the canoe without much difficulty, and was able to continue the journey little the worse for wear.

In the fireplace, the coals were dying down. Clara had crept off to bed. Catlin stepped back from his easel to look at Joe's portrait. He could see in the flickering light that it was a fine likeness, and he was pleased that he could still make a story last precisely the length of time it took to paint a portrait.

Long after midnight he climbed the stairs to bed, after wishing Joe goodby and good luck, for his friend was leaving soon for Mexico. There were no bad dreams that night. Months later, when the news came of Joe's execution by the Mexicans, the nightmares would return for a time.

But now Catlin had another dream. The collection he had risked so much for should belong to all the American people. The government would see, when he laid it all out on exhibition, that it was a priceless treasure, a record of the country's original inhabitants, that no one would ever be able to duplicate. The government would—it *must*—purchase the collection and place it in a national museum for all Americans to enjoy forever!

The artist needed time to think. Once again, he sealed rolls of canvas in watertight metal cylinders, ground a fresh supply of pigments and cleaned his firearms. This time, he struck off in a new direction, toward what he was to call "classic ground."

The sacred quarry was a strange place. Catlin was not a superstitious man, but he sensed something almost unnatural here, something that disturbed him but thrilled him at the same time.

141

Thomas Gilcrease Institute

THE SACRED PIPESTONE QUARRY
1836

Indians of all tribes made
the bowls of their peace
pipes from the dark red
stone quarried here in
southwestern Minnesota. In
1836, George Catlin col-
lected some samples of the
soft, warm, "soapy" stone
and when he sent them to be
analyzed, they proved to
be a new mineral, unknown
to science. Geologists call it
"Catlinite."

It was ordinary enough to look at: there were sheer outcroppings of red sandstone and granite here and there, and beneath them stretched a dry field where Indians were laboriously hacking chunks of red stone out of the ground. Not far away, he could see the familiar prairie and the familiar flat horizon. There was little to mark this place or set it apart from the vastness of the grasslands around it. Yet Catlin knew at once that this place *was* different. It seemed to have a power of its own. Even the air seemed different.

Time and space made their own rules here. Recent memories and even present lifetimes seemed insignificant somehow. His zig-zag voyage across the storm-tossed Great Lakes from Buffalo through Seault Ste. Marie to Green Bay, and down the winding Fox and Wisconsin Rivers to the Falls of Saint Anthony might just as well have happened to someone else, for in this place legends were more real than facts.

Since June, Catlin had been on the move. Leaving Clara with her family, he had headed west for the last time, first by steamer and then by canoe, visiting the woodland Indians, Menominees, Winnebagos, Chippewas, traversing many pine-ringed lakes until, on August 17, he had arrived at the cool, deep blue Minnesota River. With him was a genial Englishman named Robert Wood, and their destination was the sacred pipestone quarry 175 miles southwest of Fort Snelling.

This quarry was the source of stone from which calumets, or peace pipes, were made. Since the first coming of the Indians, the place had belonged to all tribes, and was considered by every Indian the holiest ground on the continent. They might hate each other bitterly in times of war but here, Catlin knew, men of all tribes always came in peace.

Catlin had always wanted to visit the quarry, and so when he met up with Mr. Wood, traveling alone and unburdened by a fixed schedule, it was a simple matter to set their course in this direction.

Their only mistake was that they spoke openly of their plans. Word quickly reached the Sioux that two white men were looking for the pipestone quarry. From long, unhappy experience, they jumped to the conclusion that Catlin and his companion must be government men in disguise. When Wood and Catlin reached LeBlanc's trading post at Traverse des Sioux, they beached their canoe and went inside to bargain for horses, as the rest of the journey would take them overland. There the Sioux were waiting for them.

"We look at you," said one, "and we see that you are Che-mo-ke-mon captains (white men officers): we know that you have been sent by your Government, to see what that place is worth, and we think the white people want to buy it."

Another joined in. "We have seen always that the white people, when they see anything in our country that they want, send officers to value it, and then if they can't buy it, they will get it some other way."

"We know that the whites are like a great cloud that rises in the East, and will cover the whole country. We know that they will have all our lands; but if ever they get our Red Pipe Quarry they will have to pay very dear for it."

"We love to go to the Pipe Stone, and get a piece for our pipes; but we ask the Great Spirit first. If the white men go to it, they will take it out, and not fill up the holes again, and the Great Spirit will be offended."

Catlin spoke up. "My friends, you have entirely mistaken us; we are no officers, nor are we sent by any one. The white men do not want the red pipe . . . they don't use pipes—they don't know how to smoke them. . . . I give you great credit for the course you are taking to preserve and protect it; and I will do as much as any man to keep white men from taking it away from you. . . . But we have started to go and see it; and we cannot think of being stopped."

Before the Indians left, they issued a warning: "White men!

Your words are very smooth; you have some object in view or you would not be so determined to go. You have no good design, and the quicker you turn back the better; there is no use of talking any more about it. If you think best to go, try it."

But when the horses were ready, the Indians were nowhere to be seen. Catlin and Wood galloped westward across the plains, determined not to let the Indians see their fear. But each time they had to enter a grove of trees or pass through a narrow ravine, the thought of a sudden ambush rode with them.

Why the Sioux decided to leave them alone, they never found out. Perhaps the Indians believed the white men's story in the end; perhaps not. At any rate the two companions, though they knew they were being watched, finished their journey without any more interference.

Now they were camped on a hill overlooking the quarry. Their supper was finished. Mr. Wood was strumming softly on his guitar, and Catlin was stretched out near the fire with his notebook open on the ground in front of him. All the legends he had ever been told about this place came back to him with a rush: legends of brotherhood, of loyalty and of peace. The words seemed to write themselves, and his pencil was still flying across the pages long after the sun had set and the first stars were beginning to twinkle in the twilight.

As Catlin labored to put these legends into writing, he came close to believing them. Here on this little bluff overlooking the holy ground, he understood the Indians in a new way: not from the outside, as a painter of painted faces and beautiful garments, but from the *inside,* almost as if, for that brief moment, he was one of them.

In the days that followed, the feeling stayed with him. He sketched and painted the scene from every angle—though, out of respect, he never entered the quarry itself. He took long rides through swaying grasses sprinkled with goldenrod and sky-blue bergamot, always returning to sit for hours beside the stream, listening to the whiz of dragonflies and the distant clink of the quarriers' tools.

Over and over, he asked himself whether the pipestone quarry, and what it stood for, could be saved. How long would the legends be allowed to permeate this air? How long until the Indians would be driven away from this small piece of land where, in all the world, the stone of peace was found? For when that day came, there would be no more peace—Catlin was certain of it.

There was still a chance, one chance. The white men in the East who made the policies and wrote the treaties might still listen to reason. They might still be open-minded enough and generous enough to leave the Indians in peace. It was already too late to do much east of the Mississippi, for the Indian lands had nearly all been seized. But west of the Mississippi, surely there was enough room for everyone. A great national park could be set aside where the Indians and the buffalo could be safe from outside interference. They could live and roam there as always in the past, free, proud and independent. No fur traders would be allowed to corrupt them. No missionaries would try to degrade the beliefs of their ancestors. There would be no more smallpox, no whiskey, no shoddy goods offered for the skins of wild animals.

The chance was slim, perhaps. But Catlin was determined to work for this dream, even if it took the rest of his life. It was time to stop his wanderings and get to work. It would mean putting aside his paints and turning his steps eastward—perhaps forever. He would have to leave behind his Indian friends and his well-worn moccasins. From now on, he would be a new kind of missionary, perhaps even a politician. He would have to sleep under slate roofs cut off from the stars at night, and his clothes would have to come from the dark shops of city tailors. Yet, despite all this, Catlin found himself looking forward eagerly to the next phase of his life.

҂҂҂҂Death of
a Warrior҂҂҂

SEPTEMBER 23, 1837. CLINTON HALL WAS IN
an uproar. With only two days left until opening time, half of
Catlin's packages and crates were still to be unpacked. Carpenters banged away, while the artist and his helpers super-
vised the installation of new gaslight fixtures. Handbills and
tickets still hadn't arrived from the printer. Someone was out
scouring New York for a set of wooden poles for the huge Crow
tepee. There weren't enough chairs for the audience, and the
proprietor of the building wouldn't bring more unless Catlin
settled his bill.

For one panicky moment, Catlin thought of postponing his
opening. There was still so much to do, and so little time. But

the day's papers were already out on the streets, carrying his
advertisement:

CATLIN'S INDIAN GALLERY

Opens for exhibition on Monday Evening, the 25th instant
and will be continued each evening. . . . In the lecture
room of Clinton Hall. There will be several hundred Portraits exhibited, as well as splendid costumes—Paintings of
their villages—Dances—Buffalo Hunts—Religious Ceremonies, etc. Collected by himself, among the wildest tribes of
America, during an absence from this city of seven years.
Mr. Catlin will be present at all of these exhibitions, giving
illustrations and explanations in the form of a Lecture. . . .
Each admission 50 cents.

There could be no postponement, so, tired as he was, Catlin
turned back to his work.

On the walls of the lecture hall, the Indian Gallery was
slowly taking shape. Under the flickering lamps, the portraits
of Catlin's old friends gleamed row upon row upon row. One
Horn and Four Bears and Black Hawk and Buffalo Bull and
Bloody Hand and Big Elk, famous warriors, medicine men and
squaws hung there in all their finery. In another part of the
room, the strange, rugged landscapes were going up, so close
together that their wide black frames almost touched, the pale
greens of the high prairies seeming to flow and blend into the
dark greens of the deep northern forests. The hall was alive
with buffalo and deer, and the painted warriors and women of
forty-eight Indian tribes fought, and hunted, and danced across
the walls. When the last picture was put in place, the gallery
covered all four walls of the big room from the ceiling almost to
the floor. Besides the 494 paintings, there were drums, spears,
robes, pipes, bows, dresses, clubs and medicine bags hanging
everywhere. And in a place of honor stood the brilliantly decorated white Crow tepee.

Finally the work was finished: the carpenters had gone, the

149

chairs were in place, the gas lights burned brightly, the tickets were ready. Catlin, strolling about the hall for one last look, wondered about those tickets. Who would buy them? Would anyone come?

He paused in front of the full-length portrait of Four Bears. The people *must* come. They *must* understand.

Four Bears was dead. Smallpox, the white man's pestilence, had visited Four Bears' village in July, killing all but thirty-eight of the Mandans.

Catlin had not heard the news; it would be nearly a year before word of the fatal epidemic could travel down the Missouri and the Ohio and across the mountains to New York. But he had foreseen such tragedies many times, and in his lecture that night he would speak out strongly against the evils of the fur trade. He would explain that stealing and murder were white men's practices, and that Indians only broke the law when white men egged them on. He would describe the humiliating surrender of Black Hawk, and plead for better government policies. He would propose his idea of a national park set aside for Indians, the only solution he could see to the coming extinction of all the tribes.

But he would also have to entertain his audience, to amuse and fascinate them with his tales. During the past summer, he had tried out his lecture in Utica and Albany, N.Y. There he quickly learned that his audiences believed all Indians were dirty and treacherous. They came to his performance expecting to hear about bloody massacres, but instead, Catlin pointed to the Indians' virtue and high-mindedness, and blamed the white community squarely for the Indians' lapses. People who came to be lectured *to* resented being lectured *at,* Catlin found. So tonight he would call on his talent for story-telling. He would tell funny stories as well as grim ones. Perhaps if he could make them laugh, he could make them think soberly and sadly, too.

National Collection of Fine Arts, Smithsonian Institution

Soon after Catlin left Fort Moultrie with his portrait of Osceola, the rest of the Seminole prisoners were taken to Arkansas, where they were to join their kinsmen near Fort Gibson. King Philip, who had been "a man of great notoriety and distinction in his time," died on the march.

As the hour of eight approached, Catlin put on his silk hat and went outside to greet his visitors.

Once on the lecture platform, the artist relaxed for the first time in weeks. The preparations had all been made. Everything was in place. There was nothing more to be done, except to delve into his seven years' first-hand experience of races and customs no one sitting there had ever seen or dreamt of. As he talked on, he was aware of the faces below him, at first gay as at a theater or circus, then becoming grave and attentive. From time to time he heard laughter and applause, and he knew they were his. At the end, they stood up cheering and clapping, then swarmed eagerly around him asking questions and voicing their enthusiasm.

Each night the scene repeated itself; and each time the audience was larger. Those who didn't arrive early had to stand in the back of the room. Soon it was clear that the Indian Gallery would have to be moved to a larger hall. In October Catlin put the portraits and dresses and all the other artifacts back into their crates and moved them to Stuyvesant Institute on Broadway. In three hectic days, the whole Gallery was reinstalled and the series of lectures began again. As the word spread, Catlin's audiences continued to grow. And the newspapers, which had ignored the first opening, now were paying serious attention to what Catlin was saying.

Long before sunset November 1, a crowd began to form outside Stuyvesant Institute, and by eight o'clock fifteen hundred tickets had been sold, at double the usual price. The news had gone out: Catlin's Indian Gallery was to be visited that night by the great Sauk chief Keokuk, his wife, and twenty of his tribesmen. Every newspaper in town sent a reporter, and every New Yorker, it seemed, wanted a ticket.

The lucky ones who were able to get into the hall came away

feeling their dollars had been well spent; it was an evening New York would talk about for months. The Indians entered happily into the evening's entertainment, interrupting Catlin's remarks from time to time and enjoying themselves famously. When Catlin brought out a portrait of Keokuk himself, grandly posing on horseback, they broke into a piercing yell.

Keokuk, attempting to apologize, rose and spoke directly to the audience. "My friends, I hope you will pardon my men for making so much noise, as they were very much excited by seeing me on my favorite war horse, which they all recognized in a moment."

After this exciting evening, Catlin's name was made. People began to flock to Stuyvesant Institute to see the paintings—and to see what further surprises were in store. When other Plains delegations passed through New York on the way to Washington, he made a point of inviting them, too, and the crowds kept on coming.

When old Putnam Catlin came to New York and finally saw what his son had accomplished, he forgot all his Yankee reserve. For many years he had worried and waited while his son, self-taught and undefended, roamed the savage wilderness. Now he could see with his own eyes what the rest of New York was seeing: a huge, brilliant, extraordinary display of priceless paintings made by one of the most unusual men of his time. To George's young brother Francis, Putnam Catlin boasted unashamedly: "It will please all of you to learn that I have full confidence in the successful career of your brother George— you can hardly imagine the splendor of his Gallery as exhibited in New York . . . I have never been acquainted with a man more popular than he is among all classes. . . ."

And, just before Christmas, Clara presented George with a baby daughter, Libby, blue-eyed and affectionate like herself. No one could ask for more.

153

But a storm was brewing in the South. A thousand miles away, in Florida, the long-standing conflict between the Indians and the slave-owning planters had flared into war. Now, at the moment of George Catlin's triumph, the New York newspapers carried an announcement of the capture of Osceola, the famous Seminole leader. Riding toward a parley with a white flag of truce, the young hero had been tricked and captured by soldiers and, in chains, had been taken to Fort Moultrie, a broken man. The reports hinted darkly that Osceola might not live long in captivity.

On January 1, 1838, Catlin closed his Gallery at the peak of its popularity, and in a few days he was on a steam packet bound for Charleston, determined to paint a portrait of Osceola before it was too late.

For years the U. S. government had been trying to move the Seminole Indians off their lands in Georgia, Florida, and Alabama, and for years, the Indians had resisted. At first the government used force: it sent whole battalions of troops to do battle with the Seminoles, and finally chased them down into the Florida peninsula. But the Indians took to hiding themselves deep in the Everglades, knowing that the white man could not find them. Then, under Osceola's fiery leadership, they counter-attacked by night, escaping again into the alligator swamps before morning.

Then the government came to the Seminoles with documents. The documents promised to give the Indians a new place to live in the West, where they would no longer be hunted and chased by soldiers or land-greedy white men. Most of the Seminole chieftains were impressed by the pieces of paper—although they could not read them. But Osceola had plunged his knife into one such document, vowing never to give up the fight.

Now, Osceola's resistance was over. At Fort Moultrie, shut away from the sky, he was suffering his illness and humiliation calmly. Though pain showed in his eyes, Catlin thought him one of the most striking-looking men he had ever seen, part Seminole, part Creek and part Scots. Stoically he posed for Catlin's brush, dressed in his silver necklace and handsome sash.

Many people would later say this portrait of Osceola was George Catlin's masterpiece. But even before Catlin could show it to his public in New York—while he was still on his way home, in fact—the brave warrior died.

When Catlin reopened the Gallery, with the portrait of Osceola prominently displayed, the crowds were bigger and more admiring than ever. The death of Osceola proved beyond a doubt that Catlin was right, and that the nation's Indian policy was wrong.

Catlin decided this was his time to move. It was time to take his exhibition to Washington. It was time to present his case to the government.

City of the White Fathers

WASHINGTON, D. C. WAS STILL A SMALL TOWN in 1838; the streets were filled with mud when it rained and choked with dust when it didn't. And the only really grand buildings were the White House and the Capitol. Sheep and other livestock grazed on the Capitol lawns, and in summer weather, disease always struck, for the city's sewage ran down the center of town in an open ditch.

Everyone complained of the crude living accommodations. The hotels were miserable, they said, the restaurants could kill you, and the summer heat and smells were almost unbearable. Each year with the coming of spring Washingtonians turned their thoughts to getting out of town before the hot weather set in.

156

Arriving in April with his parcels and crates, Catlin set off through the rain-sodden streets of Washington to rent a suitable hall for the display of the Indian Gallery. He wanted the very best showplace in the capital. All the important officials of the government would be coming to see the gallery. No expense could be spared now, for the most important thing was to impress these distinguished visitors. They must be so impressed that the government would buy the collection for the American people. Congress was still in session, and there was a bill already being considered by the Indian Affairs Committee. Catlin was sure that all Congress needed was a little nudge. And nudge them he would.

The "Old Theater" downtown was the best Washington could offer, though after New York it seemed far from elegant. Catlin hired the hall, printed twenty-five hundred catalogues and sent out invitations to all officialdom.

The crowd on opening night was large and festive. After the well-dressed dignitaries and their wives strolled about the theater admiring the paintings and fingering the artifacts, Catlin launched into his lecture. The audience seemed especially responsive. They laughed at the story of Catlin's narrow escape from the mosquitoes, and listened attentively to his tales of the buffalo chase and the sacred religious ceremony of the Mandans. The artist talked on and on, warming to his subject. Finally he came around to his main point.

If he had learned one thing in all his travels among the American Indians, he stated, it was that they were fair, honest, dignified, upright, deeply religious human beings—not bloodthirsty "savages." Disbelief crossed some of the faces in the audience.

Moreover, it was a wonder the Indians didn't rise up as one and turn the white man back at the frontier. Too many treaties had already been broken by the government. Many tribes were becoming bitter and disillusioned, and with good reason. The United States must change its ways—the Indians must have the respect they deserved. Now, the audience was rustling in the seats.

It is for these inoffensive and unoffending people, yet unvisited by the vices of civilized society, that I would proclaim to the world that it is time, for the honor of our country, for the honor of every citizen of the Republic, and for the sake of humanity, that our Government should raise her strong arm to save the remainder of them from the pestilence which is rapidly advancing upon them. We have gotten from them territory enough, and the country which they now inhabit is most of it too barren of timber for the use of civilized man. It affords them, however, the means and luxuries of savage life, and it is to be hoped that our Government will not acquiesce in the continued willful destruction of these happy people.

The politicians were looking at their pocket watches now. But Catlin pushed on with his plea.

Pointing to the portrait of Osceola, he reminded his guests that in all the nation, this might well be the only visual record of a great hero, a victim of white men's treachery. And over there hung the proud figure of Four Bears, dead because the government failed to put a stop to the wastage of the fur trade!

In a few short years, almost nothing would be left except these simple paintings of fallen and forgotten peoples. Could not the great government of the United States find it in its generous heart to acquire the fruits of Catlin's labor, for the sake of generations of Americans still unborn?

At last, the artist was finished. The lights went up, and the audience rose to applaud. But the applause was brief and polite—almost cool. Perhaps he did not realize it then, but Catlin should not have spoken so strongly. These people who were now hastening to their carriages would not take kindly some of his remarks. For these were the people who *made* the policies Catlin had so sharply criticized. And these were the people who would decide the fate of Catlin's Indian Gallery.

In the weeks that followed, Catlin called on members of Congress at their homes and offices. Too often they were "not at home," or "not in." The 25th Session of Congress came to a close without any action on Catlin's bill. It was too late in the year for its consideration, said the Chairman of the Indian Affairs Committee.

Then hot weather set in. No more legislation would be passed that summer, and each day attendance at the gallery dropped, as the people of Washington began to trickle out of the steaming city.

Still hopeful that Congress would act favorably at the next session, Catlin closed his Washington exhibit in July and took it—a whole carload—up the B.&O. railroad tracks to Baltimore. The Washington engagement had cost him heavily. He had paid large sums for the catalogue, and for rentals and for hired labor to hang the pictures and clean the halls. The only way to meet his growing expenses, and those of his family, was to keep on exhibiting the Gallery.

He stayed in Baltimore two weeks and then showed another fortnight in Philadelphia. In the middle of August he opened the show in Boston.

Packing and unpacking eight tons of material every few weeks was exhausting work. And Catlin was even growing tired of lecturing.

The audience always loved his colorful accounts of the Wild West, and they praised his paintings extravagantly. But he could tell, from the questions they asked, that they were not interested in what became of the Indians. They simply didn't care.

The election of 1838 came and went, but still no word from Congress. From time to time the newspapers carried rumors of impending action, and now Catlin's friends Daniel Webster and Henry Clay were actively trying to help his cause. There were letters from individual Congressmen expressing good will, but still nothing was done.

159

Royal Ontario Museum, Toronto

INDIANS AND GRIZZLIES, AROUND *1857*

Some of the subjects Catlin painted were so popular that he turned to them over and over again. He made many versions of this scene, each one a little more dramatic than the last. When this was painted, the artist was about sixty years old, but his imagination was as vivid as ever.

Money was becoming a serious problem. Ticket sales were always good, but the cost of moving from place to place ate up any profits. Now it was not just a matter of principle: not only should the government buy his collection for the sake of history —he was beginning to need the money desperately.

At last, having tried diplomacy and failed, Catlin resorted to one last weapon. If the United States did not soon make a bid, he announced, he would offer his priceless collection for sale in Europe.

There was a great public protest, as Catlin had hoped there would be. The press carried a flood of editorials all urging the government to immediate action. It was unthinkable, cried the newspapers, that such a national treasure should be lost to some foreign country.

Catlin had taken a desperate chance. If the government called his bluff, he faced financial disaster.

And in the summer of 1839, while Catlin awaited yet another convening of Congress, an unexpected blow fell. Until now, Catlin had always known that he could fall back on his old profession of portrait painting. He could always eke out a living making pictures of wealthy people, wherever he chose to live. But a scenery-painter named Louis Jacques Mandé Daguerre, working in a cluttered Paris studio, had discovered a process that would nearly put portrait painting to an end. On a silvered sheet of copper, Daguerre was able to produce an imitation of reality so perfect that any painter's work seemed crude by comparison. The moment Samuel Morse and Mathew Brady stepped off the Paris boat in New York with Daguerre's new device in their luggage, the era of photography had begun. In no time, daguerreotyping was taken up by every painter who knew a little about chemistry, and by every chemist who knew a little about art. Portrait painting in America would never be the same again.

Now Catlin lowered his price: in public, he said he would accept $60,000 for his Indian Gallery. Privately, he admitted that he would take almost any reasonable offer at all. Still no word came from Washington. The truth was that Congressmen were elected by white men—mostly white men living in rural areas. There were few "Indian-lovers" among this voting public, and any politician who favored spending taxpayers' money on a bunch of pictures of "savages" was asking for defeat. Nevertheless, Catlin's friends promised to keep his cause alive as long as there was any hope.

So the government had called Catlin's bluff, and Daguerre's invention had cut off his last line of retreat.

Catlin had no choice left. On November 25, 1839, George, his nephew Burr, and his assistant, Daniel Kavanaugh, left New York with eight tons of priceless paintings and Indian artifacts, on the steam packet *Roscius*. On the deck, in a huge iron cage, rode two full-grown grizzly bears which Catlin had somehow obtained from the Rocky Mountains, "not only the heaviest and most awkward part of my freight, but altogether the most troublesome."

They were bound for Liverpool, then London. It was now or never.

National Collection of Fine Arts, Smithsonian Institution

Catlin painted this nine-year-old Seminole boy in London, against an imaginary Florida backdrop. The boy had been adopted and brought to London by a Dr. Welch, after his capture by United States troops in an Indian skirmish.

~~~~~Queen Victoria's London~~~~~

THE PACKET-SHIP *ROSCIUS* CROSSED THE AT-
lantic in six weeks. By 1839 standards, it was a wonderfully
swift crossing, but to George Catlin, the days and nights sometimes seemed endless. Winter gales whipped the sea into a fury
and sent an icy spray dashing across the decks. As the engines
shuddered and the ship pitched over the huge waves, George
sat wretchedly in his cabin or writhed on his bunk, hideously
seasick, longing for Clara.

On deck the grizzly bears howled and tore at their cage, frantic to escape the never-ending motion. Burr, the artist's big,
strapping young nephew, did what he could to help his uncle,
and Daniel, the Irish "Man Friday," make the bears as comfortable as possible.

165

On good days Catlin welcomed the gaiety and elegance of the ship and its passengers. As long as the seas were calm, his optimism soared. "To Cross the Ocean," he wrote, "is but to sit down in a fine hotel, and pass the time among good company." On such days he could look ahead and see himself and his Indian Gallery showered with honor and fame. Lords and Ladies, Dukes and Earls would beat a path to his door.

And Catlin's extravagant dream seemed to be coming true as soon as the ship landed. Whenever he made a friend, he kept it, and there on the dock to greet him was no less than the Honorable Charles A. Murray, Master of the Queen's Household, who had traveled with him for a time on the Mississippi. Poor Daniel was put in charge of finding lodgings for the howling bears, while Catlin went on to London to arrange exhibition space.

Murray began at once to introduce Catlin to London society, making sure that the artist met "everybody." Invitations began to appear at the artist's door, delivered by liveried servants.

The grizzly bears, meanwhile, proved too much for the English people. Terrifying news swept the country. Rumor had it that the "two huge monsters imported from the Rocky Mountains had scales like alligators, with long spears of real flint at the ends of their tails; that they made nothing of eating paving-stones when they were hungry, and that in Liverpool they had escaped, and were traveling to the north, and demolishing all the inhabitants of Lancashire as they went along." Actually Daniel had them well in hand.

By the end of January, although Catlin had been in London only a few weeks, he had already spent nearly two thousand dollars. His three large exhibition rooms in Egyptian Hall, Piccadilly, were well-located and well-designed, but the rental was exorbitant. And the splendor of London social life meant visits to expensive tailors, and (something unknown in America)

166

it meant having a different hat for each kind of occasion or time of day. Moreover, he had Burr and Daniel to feed and house, as well as the grizzly bears, who finally had to be boarded at the London Zoo, at considerable expense.

But there was no time to think about expenses now, for there was the huge exhibition to be hung and preparations for the opening to be made. For nearly a month they worked, Burr and Daniel tending to the countless details of arranging the show, printing the handbills, and arranging lights and chairs at Egyptian Hall. Catlin took care of publicity, making his circuit of London society, stirring up the curiosity and enthusiasm of the city's great men and ladies.

The money and time were well spent, for the opening was greeted by the finest, richest, and most influential audience ever. And the reporters raved as never before over both the artist and his achievement.

When he wrote to his parents that February, George was glowing with excitement:

London. *17th Feby 1840*

My Dear Parents,

. . . You will all rejoice to hear that I am well, although almost half crazy with the bustle and excitement I have been continually under in this great and splendid city—amongst nobody but strangers, and those of the most difficult and particular kind to deal with. I have had the trembling excitements and fears to contend with which beset & besiege a green horn from the backwoods when making his Debut & his bow to the most polite & fastidious part of the whole world—I have kept as cool as possible—have pursued steadily & unflinchingly my course, and have at last succeeded in making what they call here, a *"decided hit."*

Months went by, and the crowds continued to flock to Egyptian Hall. Gradually, however, Catlin was coming to realize that even when every seat was filled, his income was only barely

CATLIN AND HIS PARTY
IN THEIR CANOE
CONFRONTED BY BEARS
ON SHORE, AFTER *1838*

To make his Indian Gallery more exciting, Catlin added a number of crowd-pleasing "Wild West" adventures to the scenes on his walls. Here, he shows Ba'tiste, Bogard and himself trading threats with a family of grizzlies on the Missouri River.

larger than his expenses. And where was Clara? And little Libby, and the new baby, named for her mother, that Catlin had not yet seen? He waited eagerly for their arrival all through the beautiful London spring, looking forward to sharing his glory with them. At last, in June, they came.

Clara was enchanted with London, and soon she was caught up, like all of London, in the gaiety of young Queen Victoria's early years. As George wrote his proud parents:

My faithful friend the Hon. C. A. Murray, who had called on Clara the day after she arrived, and who is Master of the Queen's Household, politely presented us a couple of tickets admitting us to the Grand Hall in Buckingham Palace on the day of the Queen's Drawing Room or Levee so that Clara had a perfect view of Her Majesty & the Prince, as well as the rest of her household & attendants, as they descended the grand stairway from the Throne Room in full dress and took their carriages for St. James' Palace, where the Levee was held, & which is about a half a mile distant from Buckingham Palace. Then, through the politeness of another friend of mine, who has charge of St. James' Palace, (with his good lady) seats were prepared for us in this grand avenue or hall or that, to which we instantly repaired, and there had a full view of the whole procession of Ladies & Lords, of Duchesses & Dukes, Princesses and Princes, in full Court Dress—with laces & plumes & glittering diamonds as they were alighting from their splendid carriages & entering the Drawing Room of the palace.

This scene to Clara was no less gratifying than it was for me, & thus she had the good fortune, in one day, to enter two Palaces & see the Queen & all her court & all the fashionables who flounced about and glittered in it!

But all too soon it was the "dull season" in London; the fashionable public were all at their summer homes in the country.

Hoping to drum up some new interest, Catlin hired a group of English boys to put on Indian costumes and perform Indian rituals and dances. He also ordered expensive new gaslight fixtures. Even Burr, who was over six feet tall and very blonde, pitched in to help, shaving his head like a Pawnee and parading the streets of London in buckskin and bears'-teeth. Once George, Clara and Burr appeared at a ball in fine Indian outfits and full makeup, speaking only through an "interpreter." It was an effective way to advertise; the audiences did improve. Feeling sure that big crowds would return in the fall, Catlin signed another lease on Egyptian Hall, and devoted his time to Clara and the children, and to his great new project, a book describing his adventures in the American wilderness.

Though Americans, reading about Catlin's triumphant opening in London, assumed he was making a fortune, the artist was having a hard time making ends meet. There were seven mouths to feed now, for Clara had brought with her the children's nurse, Bridget. George was also sending money regularly to his father, and repaying a loan that he owed to Clara's brother.

Catlin re-doubled his effort to finish his book and to enlarge his audiences, for soon there would be eight in the household. That summer a third daughter was born, and like many another English baby, she was christened Victoria, after England's adored young Queen. George worked night and day on the book. When it was finished, *Letters and Notes on the Manners, Customs, and Condition of the North American Indians* contained five-hundred-thirty pages and four hundred illustrations made from his own sketches.

It was an exciting book, the first and best of its kind, touching on a world never before described so vividly in print. Catlin had delved into his overflowing and travel-stained notebooks and into his crowded memory, to create a fascinating account of life far beyond the western frontier. The two volumes were full of lively stories about the Indians he had met and come to admire during eight years of travel. They also contained a wealth of scientific information: geology, botany, paleontology and zoology all came under discussion.

But above all, the book was a plea for understan'ing. Over and over the author appealed to his readers' sense of morality and justice.

The critics said *Letters and Notes* deserved to be a best-seller. And it was. The first printing was bought up by eager readers within a few weeks. A second, third, and fourth edition followed. It is still being printed today.

Catlin made little money from the successful book at first, however, because he had published it at his own expense. It would take time to earn back the nearly $10,000 the venture had cost him. But there was no doubt in his mind that in the near future the book would prove to have been worth his while.

Catlin later said that he could not have completed the book without the gentle presence of Clara, "who, though delicate and tender, had been, during the last three years of my rambles in the Indian wilds, my indefatigable companion." George, Clara and the little girls were now enjoying their first real home, Rose Cottage, snug among the gardens of suburban London.

The book appeared in October, 1841, but though it was an overnight "hit," by winter it was clear that the big crowds of the previous year weren't coming back to Egyptian Hall. Rather than sit idly until profits from the book came in, Catlin packed up his paintings and costumes and drums and spears and utensils and artifacts, and set off in search of new audiences in the smaller cities of the British Isles. It was an exhausting tour. He went to Rugby, Edinburgh, Manchester, Leeds, Glasgow, Belfast and Dublin, spending money he could ill afford, and his crowds, though enthusiastic, were small. England was in the midst of a severe financial crisis, and these working-class towns had been hard hit. Queen Victoria even had to issue a half-farthing coin, because some people were too poor to spend a whole farthing at one time.

In addition, England was becoming almost violently anti-

American. Catlin had not noticed it in the polite company of London society, but out in the provinces he found that people hated Americans bitterly for aiding Canada in her struggles against the Crown.

Catlin returned to Rose Cottage little richer than when he left. There seemed no point in staying on in England, he said. They might as well begin packing up to go home to America.

Plans were made, boat tickets were reserved, and Clara set happily about preparing for the journey. Over the summer, old Putnam Catlin had died, and so had Clara's own father. Home never seemed so far away to her as it did during the months that followed, with George away on tour and family correspondence so slow and unreliable.

But Clara was never to see her beloved family again, for now, in the early spring of 1843, a strange and fatal new series of events began to unfold.

Two weeks before the family was to sail, an American named Arthur Rankin materialized out of nowhere, on a Liverpool dock. With him were nine full-blooded Ojibwa Indians, whom Rankin planned to place on public exhibition. This mysterious person sent Catlin a note, proposing that they go into partnership. Catlin was appalled by the idea of the exhibit, particularly because he was afraid that the Indians might end up being gazed at like wild animals in a carnival. And he did not like the sound of the American stranger. "I have always been opposed to the plan of bringing Indians abroad on speculation," he replied. But for the sake of the Indians' welfare, he agreed. "As they are in the country, I shall, as the friend of the Indians under all circumstances, feel an anxiety to promote their views and success in any way I can." He ordered his belongings unpacked and signed another lease on Egyptian Hall. The only condition was that Rankin himself must be responsible for the Indians when they were outside Egyptian Hall.

173

National Collection of Fine Arts, Smithsonian Institution

After the Ojibwas left, a band of Iowas took their place in Catlin's touring Indian Gallery. This handsome warrior from the prairies lost first his infant son and then his wife to the deadly diseases of "civilization."

Briefly, the London audiences responded. They returned to the Hall again, to see the "real live American Indians," but soon their enthusiasm turned to ice. Rankin, despite his promise, allowed the Ojibwas to run wild in the streets, drinking and brawling, and carousing on the rooftops. Queen Victoria invited a large party of guests for a command performance, but as Charles Dickens wrote, the Indians were an insult to the Royal Presence, "squatting and spitting on the table . . . mere animals and wretched creatures."

For the first time in his life, Catlin's truthfulness was questioned. Were *these* the noble heroes Catlin had written of, painted and praised? The press, once so friendly, now accused Catlin of deliberate falsehood and implied that it was *his* fault the Indians were disrupting the peacefulness of London.

After three months of scandal and disaster Rankin pulled his "exhibits" out of Catlin's show. Renting rooms in the very same building, Rankin set up his own "Wild Indian" show.

There were almost no visitors at all now; no one would have anything to do with the "frauds" and "charlatans" in Egyptian Hall. Then Catlin published a portfolio of twenty-five large, handsome Wild West pictures, and this helped to restore some of his former respectability. And he had a baby son, at last. Of all his children, little George quickly became his father's favorite.

Certainly it was time to go home now. There was nothing more to be gained in England.

Once again, Catlin arranged passage home for his household and his freight. Once again, Clara began the happy task of packing the steamer trunks. And once again, a tribe of traveling Indians appeared out of the blue to prevent their departure.

This time, however, the circumstances were altogether different. The Indians were tall, fine-looking Iowas, and among them were White Cloud and Walking Rain, whose portraits

G. Catlin. London. 18

Thomas Gilcrease Institute

TROUPE OF INDIANS IN LONDON, *1844*

The rigors of living thousands of miles from home show on the faces of these Ojibwas who joined Catlin's exhibition in London.

hung in Catlin's gallery. Their escort was a Mr. G. H. C. Melody, another old friend. They greeted Catlin with his Iowa nickname, "Chippehola," and begged the artist to let them dance in his exhibition. Catlin saw this as his last chance to show the people of England some "real" Indians from the Plains, and to prove that the Plains Indians were everything he had said them to be.

So, once again, Catlin signed his name to a lease on Egyptian Hall, and once again the advertisements were printed and hand-bills sent out. And once again, with a heavy heart, Clara un-packed.

This time, the people of London were deeply impressed. The Earl of Beaconfield, Disraeli, invited the whole troupe to his home, where they behaved like the noblemen they were.

On fine days they danced and whooped and galloped horses in the Vauxhall Gardens amusement park beside the Thames River. Here in the summer sunshine they re-enacted the sports and dances and hunts of the Lower Missouri. And if the nobility were out-of-town, Catlin was content, for the whole populace of London could come and enjoy the spectacle.

But the English summer was short. Soon the air turned chilly and the warm sun disappeared behind an ever-thickening gray fog. A short tour of the smaller cities ended in sadness, for two of the Iowas died in Liverpool. One of them, the son of Little Wolf, was only a baby. But Mr. Melody and most of the Iowas were having a wonderful time; they wanted to go on with their tour—to Paris, and perhaps to other great cities in Europe.

In December, 1844, Clara wrote to her sister-in-law that they would soon be leaving England. And when April came, George, Clara, the four children, the servants, the eight tons of baggage and the Iowas and Mr. Melody did leave England. But it was eastward they headed, across the English Channel, not home-ward across the Atlantic.

Beginnings & Endings

PARIS WAS FULL OF PROMISE IN THE SPRING of 1845. After the smoke and jumble of bustling London, the French capital with its wide avenues and majestic spaces seemed to belong to another world. April flowers were bursting from their buds, and under a fine, clean rain the trees along the Champs-Elysées were turning from winter brown to a joyous green.

Completely captivated by the city, and already feeling at ease with the new language, Catlin found rooms for his family, and rented a large hall on the fashionable Rue St. Honoré for his exhibition. Now that he had become acquainted with London nobility, it was an easy matter to arrange a meeting with Queen

179

Victoria's cousin, King Louis Philippe. To publicize his arrival, Catlin hired a horse-drawn omnibus and paraded the Iowas through the city in all their finery. Traffic came to a standstill while Paris gazed dumfounded at the magnificent *"Peaux Rouges"* and *"Sauvages horribles."*

Catlin had been only a baby when the young Duke of Orleans passed through Wilkes-Barre on his way to the Mississippi River, but George had heard the story over and over again as he grew up. Now the young Duke had become Louis Philippe, King of the French. Catlin felt completely at ease with the monarch, and as they strolled the gardens of the Tuileries together, they had much to discuss. After nearly fifty years, the King's memories of the American West had grown dim, but with Catlin at his side, the two recalled the faraway landscape as if it were still before them.

Speaking to the Iowas, the King said: "Tell these good people that the Queen and I are glad to see them. That I have been in many of the wigwams of the Indians in America, when I was a young man, and they treated me everywhere with kindness, and I love them for it."

By the third of June, the *Galerie Indienne* was ready for its public opening. All the great men and women of the day attended—Victor Hugo the poet and playwright, George Sand the novelist, and the leading scientist of Europe, seventy-six-year-old Baron Alexander von Humboldt, who took an instant liking to George Catlin and the Iowas.

Catlin was in his element. He was always good at beginnings, and this was the best beginning of them all.

But though the whooping, dancing Iowas were the hit of the season, they were tired and becoming more homesick every day. And when, in July, Little Wolf's wife died, they finally rebelled. Catlin and Mr. Melody begged them to stay a little longer—at least until they began to show a profit—but they were adamant. They would stay six more days, they said, in order to say farewell to all their friends in Paris. But then they were going home.

Catlin missed Melody's company, and he missed the cheerful confusion of the Iowas' comings and goings. Clara must have watched their departure with even greater sadness, for she, too, was homesick and tired. How she would have loved to sail away with them! But as always, she stayed by her husband's side. Her husband was in deep difficulty now, she knew. More than ever, he needed her and the children close by.

Perhaps if Clara had left when the Indians did, she would not have caught cold that July. She would not have developed pneumonia. And she would not have died.

All the wise men and crowned heads of Europe could not help Catlin now. What good had it been to dine out with Kings and Princes, now that his own Clara was gone?

Catlin knew now all too well that his ambition was partly to blame for Clara's death. The years of traveling in strange lands, the years spent far from her home and family, the years of packing and unpacking—she had endured them all for her husband's sake. And all those years, he had kept promising her a wonderful future that never quite came. If only he could have kept those promises!

For the first time in many years, Catlin was without a plan. His zest for publicity was gone, and he lacked enough money to go back home. At the same time, he yearned to get out of Paris, where reminders of Clara were everywhere.

So he began to roam again, as he always did when his problems became too great. He hired a nurse for his four children and planned to spend the winter in Brussels lecturing, exhibiting, and toiling over a new book. Still another troupe of visiting Indians—Canadian Ojibwas from Lake Huron—had joined up, and together they hoped for at least a modest success.

181

But Catlin's luck did not improve. In Brussels a smallpox epidemic struck the Indians before the show opened, and three of them died. The exhibition had to be cancelled, and Catlin had to spend the next few months—at a loss of some $1,700—nursing the sick Indians back to health.

Though Louis Philippe gave him a special commission, and even arranged a special exhibition of Catlin's Indian Gallery in the Louvre, nothing seemed to matter any more.

Through the help of some wealthy Americans, the miserable Indians were sent back in January, 1846, to their Canadian hunting grounds. Before they sailed, they sent Catlin a letter:

Our dear Friend:

We send you our words on paper to let you know that we are thankful for your kindness to us. You have done everything to make us happy while with you in Paris and Belgium; and as all our people know in America that you are indeed their best friend, they will be glad to hear that you have taken us into your care whilst we were in a foreign land and that while you were in a deep affliction with your own family.

Once the Indians had departed for London, Catlin rushed back to his little family in Paris. Clara's death had changed him profoundly. At fifty he was feeling his age, growing deaf, weary and bitter. His children became the most important thing in his life and he spent every possible minute with them—especially with George, the youngest.

The artist brought his paints and canvases home, so that he could be with his children while he worked. And he renewed his letter-writing campaign to members of Congress. This time he was joined by other artists in Paris, London and New York. Together and individually, they wrote letters of their own, urging an end to the delay.

We most respectfully trust that Mr. Catlin's collection may be purchased and cherished by the federal government, as a nucleus for a national museum, where American artists may freely study that bold race who once held possession of our country, and who are so fast disappearing before the tide of civilization. Without such a collection, few of the glorious pages of our early history can be illustrated, while the use made of it here by French artists, in recording upon canvas the American discoveries of their countrymen in the last century, shows its importance.

The acquisition of the collection will also secure to our country the continued services of its author, whose ambition seems to be still to labor for its enlargement, and whose ability to do so with success, and with profit to his country, we think is well attested by the collection he has made, by years of toil, and often hardship, entirely unaided by public or private patronage. And your memorialists will ever pray.

Jno. Vanderlyn,	W. B. Chambers,
Thos. P. Rossiter,	H. Willard,
Benj. Champney,	Thos. Hicks,
Wm. M. Hunt,	J. F. Kensett,
Wm. C. Allan,	C. G. Edwards.
Geo. C. Mason,	PARIS, *May 14, 1846*

As before, the motion was referred to a committee, and as before, no action was taken.

Even the King of France took pity on his friend, and offered to pay him a generous sum for a series of large pictures showing the adventures of the French explorer La Salle, who had claimed the Mississippi River for France back in the 1670's. Louis Philippe wanted these paintings to hang forever on the walls of the Louvre, as an inspiration to the French people. Catlin set to work with a will, spending longer hours than ever at his easel, for the money was needed desperately.

Then, little more than a year after Clara's death, Catlin suffered another staggering loss. Typhoid fever struck Paris in the summer of 1846. One by one, the artist and his children fell ill. Little George, not quite three years old, did not recover. Catlin would never be able to take him hunting or fishing or horseback

183

Thomas Gilcrease Institute

RATTLE SNAKE DEN
1853–54

When George Catlin was growing up on the Susquehanna River, rattlesnakes were a serious menace. One day, George and his father and the men of the valley set out to exterminate them once and for all. Stealthily they crept up to the den where the snakes lived, and when they were all out sunning themselves, the farmers attacked. George armed himself with an old musket loaded with quantities of gunpowder, fired the first shot, and became the hero of the day. Many years later, Catlin made this painting for his English patron, Sir Thomas Phillipps, who surely had never seen a rattlesnake.

riding now. His small body was sent home to be buried beside his mother in America.

Having lost the two people most dear to him in all the world, Catlin seemed to go about in a daze. He began to write a boastful book about his eight years among the crowned heads of Europe, and he went back to London, determined to sell his Indian Gallery privately, no matter to whom, and no matter at what loss. This time there were no offers. All Europe was now in the midst of political and financial turmoil; Catlin's glowing portraits of the American "savage" seemed quaint and almost old-fashioned. The "Indian craze" was over.

In the bitterness and despair that hounded him that fall, Catlin allowed himself to make a serious mistake. Though he might not have known it, many people in the United States were finally becoming aware that Indians were not just "nuisances" and "savages." Partly through Catlin's own efforts, the government—or a part of it—was beginning at last to study the peoples of the forests and plains as human beings with a deeply-rooted culture of their own.

All Catlin knew was that the House of Representatives had turned him down again and again. From his point of view, the government was the Indians' enemy. So when, late in 1846, he received a visitor named Henry R. Schoolcraft, he was in no mood to be friendly. Schoolcraft had made the trip especially to ask Catlin an important favor. He was writing a great encyclopedia describing the Indians of North America. It would be published by the government and become the official record of Indian life as of the middle of the century. And he wanted Catlin's permission to illustrate the book with copies of his paintings. At any other time, Catlin might have seen the value of such a project, and he surely would have been flattered, but at this moment he could only think of how the government had mistreated him. Firmly and none too politely, he told Schoolcraft

"No." If such a book was contemplated by the government then he, Catlin, should have credit for it.

Years later, Catlin came to regret his rudeness. It was the intensity of his pain and frustration that made him rebuff his visitor, for Catlin was known from the Great Plains to the *salons* of Paris for his gentleness and gracious manners. But the damage was done. Schoolcraft returned to America convinced that George Catlin was a highhanded egotist, and perhaps even a liar.

In less than a year, Congress made Schoolcraft official "Historiographer to the Congress." From that time on, it was Schoolcraft who was listened to in all Indian matters, not the lonely, aging painter across the Atlantic.

Schoolcraft went on with his work, but the politicians grew more anti-Indian every year. In 1847 Congressman James D. Westcott of Florida came out with a ringing denunciation of Catlin's work: "I am opposed to purchasing the portraits of savages. What great moral lesson are they intended to inculcate? I would rather see the portraits of the numerous citizens who have been murdered by Indians. I would not vote a cent for a portrait of an Indian."

On Washington's Birthday, 1848, rebellion broke out in Paris. The people of France, tired of their antiquated Parliament, and demanding to have a say in their government, stormed the capital for the second time in as many generations. Crying "We shall never get rid of Kings until we pull down the palaces," they invaded the Louvre and camped there, threatening to burn the place down.

Louis Philippe and his Queen ran for their lives to England, where Victoria gave them safety. Catlin, who was known to be their friend, found that he, too, was in danger from the rioting mobs: any friend of the King was hated almost as much as the King himself. Hastily, Catlin arranged for his huge collection

187

to be taken back to London. By the time the artist reached England, the King had already gone into seclusion. Catlin realized then that he would never be paid for the paintings the King had ordered.

In London, he re-opened his exhibition, and went into debt to have a new catalogue printed. But the "Red Men of America" were out of fashion now. Soon he would be forced to close.

He couldn't turn to Murray, for the Queen had sent him abroad. But one of the many distinguished Englishmen in Murray's circle of friends had helped before, and so Catlin went to him again.

Sir Thomas Phillipps lived in a mansion in Worcestershire, surrounded, almost deluged, by rare books and manuscripts and notes and letters of every description. He was obsessed with collecting. To him, every snippet saved from a great man's wastebasket was a treasure to be saved for future generations.

Catlin somehow assumed that his friend, the compulsive collector of documents, would want to include the American Indian in his hoard of mementos. In August the artist offered to turn his entire collection over to Sir Thomas if he would lend him six hundred pounds.

But he had misread the size of Phillipps' fortune. The Baronet was buying documents faster than his income permitted. He himself was dangerously close to bankruptcy. So, although he expressed enthusiasm for Catlin's work, Phillipps had to admit that he had no money to spare.

Catlin never gave up hope. Congress would *someday* purchase the Indian Gallery, and he could go back to America and spend the rest of his days adding to it. In February, 1849, Daniel Webster rose from his seat in the Senate and delivered a sincere, impassioned speech:

MR. PRESIDENT: The question is, whether it does not become us, as an useful thing, to possess in the United States this collection of paintings, etc., made amongst the Indian tribes? Whether it is not a case for the exercise of *large liberality*—I will not say *bounty, but policy?* These tribes, sir, that have preceded us, to whose lands we have succeeded, and who have no written memorials of their laws, their habits, and their manners, are all passing away to the world of forgetfulness. Their likeness, manners, and customs, are portrayed with more accuracy and truth in this collection by Catlin than in all the other drawings and representations on the face of the earth. Somebody in this country ought to possess this collection—that is my opinion; and I do not know who there is, or where there is to be found, any society or any individual, who, or which can, with so much propriety possess himself, or itself, of it, as the Government of the United States. For my part, then, I do think that the preservation of CATLIN's INDIAN COLLECTION in this country is an important public act. I think it properly belongs to those accumulations of historical matters respecting our predecessors on this continent, which it is very proper for the government of the United States to maintain. As I have said, this race is going into forgetfulness. They track the continuation of mankind in the present age, and call recollection back to them. And here they are better exhibited, in my judgment, better set forth and presented to the mind, and the taste and the curiosity of mankind, than in all other collections in the world. I go for this as an *American* subject—as a thing belonging to us—to our history—to the history of a race whose lands we till, and over whose obscure graves and bones we tread every day. I look upon it as a thing more appropriate for us than the ascertaining of the South Pole, or anything that can be discovered in the Dead Sea or the river Jordan. These are the grounds, sir, upon which I propose to proceed, and I shall vote for the appropriation with great pleasure.

Senator Jefferson Davis also spoke up on Catlin's behalf. Davis, as a green lieutenant, had ridden along with Catlin out of Fort Gibson on the ill-fated expedition of the First Dragoons to the Southwest. But now he was a politician, and his constituents hated the Indians for interfering with their slave economy. At the end of his speech, Davis announced that he would have to vote *against* the bill "on principle."

On February 29, the roll was called. The vote: *yeas* 23, *nays* 25. The next day there was more debate, and this time the decision was only too clear: fifteen voted to acquire Catlin's Indian Gallery for the American people, but twenty-one voted not to.

The following year Catlin went to Sir Thomas Phillipps again, and this time his friend was in a position to help. He advanced one hundred pounds and kept twenty of Catlin's paintings as security. By now, Catlin owed money to several people. In his frantic search for money, he convinced himself he would pay it all back any day, for he was deeply involved in a new speculation: he was promoting Texas real estate through something called the "Great American Land Company." For a year he made the rounds of England, calling on all his rich acquaintances, offering them windfall profits in the American West.

But by December, 1849, the bubble had burst, and Catlin had lost everything. Phillipps now began to press for his money. In desperation the artist promised him paintings, since he had no other way of fulfilling his debt. In all, he copied fifty-five of his paintings for Sir Thomas, each one being worth less than two pounds!

To support his three children Catlin borrowed still more money. He moved into a dismal little London flat where visitors could see his paintings for a shilling. He still had hopes that the American government would come to his rescue. But it was too late.

On July 20, 1852, Senator William H. Seward begged his colleagues to reconsider. In his hand he held a newspaper clipping. It said that George Catlin was in debtors' prison, and that all his paintings were about to be sold at public auction. Dramatically he read aloud the auctioneer's advertisement, and once more the politicians plunged into debate. For hours they argued the issue in the midst of a Washington heat wave. Then someone remarked that there was more pressing business at hand.

The resolution, like so many before it, was tabled.

Clara's family had been deeply worried all along about the welfare of the three little girls. So far the Gregorys had said nothing, knowing how much their father adored his children, and how much he needed them. But now they could sit by no longer. Clara's brother, Dudley Gregory, took a fast boat to England to fetch the girls. This was no life for his nieces. They must be brought home to New Jersey, where they could enjoy all the advantages that their father was unable to give them.

Dudley Gregory was a busy man. He could not stay long. George must say goodby to his three children, and say it right away.

Their father realized that Dudley was right. The girls did deserve a far better life. It would be selfish to keep them away from home any longer. One by one, he embraced them and made still another impossible promise: he said he'd soon be home again, too.

Dudley tried to help Catlin straighten out his tangled finances while he was in London. He was a reasonably wealthy man, but when he found out just how serious the artist's debts actually were, he had to make Catlin see the hard facts: Nothing short of $40,000 would save him. And this figure was not in any way a payment for the eight years of hardship in the wilderness; it was just to keep him out of jail.

Catlin pondered this as he stood on the Liverpool dock. Forlornly, he watched as the boat steamed away, carrying his precious daughters home to America. He would have given anything to be on the boat with them. But he must stay on— at least until he had raised the $40,000. Then, perhaps, he could leave.

Catlin's financial condition was well-known. Everywhere he went, his former friends avoided him. "Nice" people didn't get into debt; and if they did, they always paid up promptly. Of course, one couldn't expect an American to know that! Americans were always careless about such things.

The artist guessed that no Englishman was likely to come forward with the money, and he was right. It was an American who finally rescued him, a Philadelphia-born locomotive manufacturer named Joseph Harrison. Harrison was on his way home after working seven years on a Russian railroad project, when he heard of Catlin's plight. Rather than see a fellow American ruined, he paid the artist's debts. But in return, Catlin had to give him his entire collection. Every painting, every war bonnet, every spear and drum, every beaded Indian dress, every stick and shred of Indian material Catlin owned went to Harrison. Or almost everything. When Harrison's men came to crate up the stuff, they overlooked one small set of sketches.

With only these few sketches, Catlin went back to Paris, severely deaf now, quite alone, and semi-invalid with his old lung trouble. He spent his days in the great Reading Room of the National Library, reading and dreaming about his adventures among the Blackfeet, Crows and Sioux twenty years before.

Buried Treasure

HE WAS IN HIS LATE FIFTIES NOW. EVERY single one of his dreams had failed, and he had nothing to show for all his years of hardship. But George Catlin did not go home. Not yet. Perhaps he knew that to go home would be the final admission of defeat. He couldn't face his family and his country empty-handed.

So his stubbornness and his pride kept him on in Paris. He still had his boundless curiosity, and his talent, and his memories. And he could still dream.

The National Library might have swallowed him up for-ever. In its vast, dusty reaches, it held all the mysteries of human history. One could spend a lifetime there, exploring the creaking iron staircases and endless passageways, looking for buried secrets in the disintegrating piles of forgotten manuscripts.

But Catlin found what he was looking for, the answer to all his problems. It was, quite literally, buried treasure. It seemed that somewhere in the great Empire of Brazil, were the lost gold mines of the Spaniards, long abandoned and unknown to anyone. Two or even three hundred years earlier, the Spanish miners had been overrun by Indians. Those not massacred had fled, leaving the gold behind—and leaving behind the secret of its location. Now Catlin held in his hand an ancient document that told where these gold mines were to be found.

Suddenly the artist saw himself returning to America, a millionaire, adored again by everyone. "Nuggets of gold of all sizes appeared in my dreams," he wrote.

In no time, he was planning how he would get a mining concession from Brazil, for the "right of working the mines and *carting* the gold away."

Why not? He had no paintings to exhibit, no children to care for. There was no reason at all not to visit Brazil and have a go at it.

His friend Sir Thomas Phillipps offered him a furnished room and a place to show his work, if he cared to come back to England. But Catlin was tired of towns, and crowds, and he wanted to have done with money worries once and for all.

In a few weeks he was in Caracas, Venezuela, "on a sandy, scorching coast." His hopes high, he rode on horseback across the highlands to the Orinoco River. But then civil war broke out in Venezuela. He had to turn back. Luckily a steamer came by to carry him out the Orinoco to Georgetown, British Guiana.

In Georgetown, one day, a young Englishman named Smyth happened to look out of his hotel window, and by a fantastic coincidence, he recognized George Catlin in the busy street below, his easel set up, his paint brushes flying. Smyth had visited

Egyptian Hall many times as a child, fascinated by what he saw. He had never forgotten Catlin's face.

It didn't take long for young Smyth to make up his mind. Whatever it was the "governor" was up to here, Smyth wanted to be with him when he did it. Smyth was strong, he was eager, and he was sure he could shoot a Minié rifle better than anyone. Smyth made his way to Catlin's room, and offered his services.

Catlin thought of his own repeating rifle named "Sam" after Sam Colt, who had made it especially for him. He would enjoy showing this brash young man a thing or two. Besides, he liked the young man's style. If he didn't mind some hard work, Smyth was welcome to come along.

When Catlin left the comforts of Georgetown, he brought quite a group with him into the jungle: besides Smyth, and Catlin's half-breed guide, there was a German doctor—a student of rare plants—and *his* guide. A Spanish interpreter had been hired as well.

To get to the gold mines, they sometimes had to hack their way through dense jungle. Each step they took meant cutting vines and creepers and thickets of bamboo—or else it meant inching across treacherous swampland. The days were sweltering and the nights noisy with the unpleasant sounds of prowling animals. Mosquitoes pursued them everywhere. Only the promise of gold at the end of the trail kept them from turning back. The German botanist was soon exhausted, and his guide took him back to Georgetown.

The destination was the Tumucamache, or Crystal, or Acarai Mountains, which lay close to the Equator, far from any white settlement. It was rough, tropical country, never fully explored or mapped. People had tried to map the region from time to time, but not all of them had returned.

Because of the tragic events in London, Catlin was traveling under an assumed name, and with a passport that he knew would not stand close scrutiny. So they could expect no help from officials either in Guiana or Brazil should they run into trouble. But Catlin and Smyth kept on, their horses doing most of the work as they crossed quicksand and muddy riverbeds.

They slogged on and on, often losing their way, but following compass directions as well as they could. From time to time, they saw traces of gold in the streams. But they pushed ahead, searching for the *real* gold, the gold that would make them rich; the gold they would *cart* away.

The streambeds were littered with gleaming stones—not gold, but more beautiful in their own way. Catlin would stroll along the beaches, cracking open the prettiest pebbles with his hammer. Then he would moisten them in his mouth to bring out the color. Indians in the isolated villages came to know Catlin as the "Stone Eater."

Too soon, the "prospectors" realized they had overshot their target. A few days' march brought them out empty-handed, at Belém on the Amazon.

Catlin still had a serious case of "gold fever" and was determined to try again. Smyth decided not to come along this time; he liked Belém, and wanted to go into business there. Instead, Catlin engaged one Caesar Bolla, a six-foot-two former slave, who had run away from his master in Havana. George, with his false passport, and Caesar, the fugitive, were joined by a Spanish rancher who asked to be called "Senor Novello," though that was not his real name. This trio of near-outlaws was determined to succeed. They equipped themselves in the most professional manner (they thought) with "a large tin pan from 'Senora Novello's' pantry, for washing gold, and a heavy hammer for breaking the rocks, and a cold chisel for cutting the nuggets which we might find too large to be transported entire!"

But after two weeks of hard travel over land and water, and within sight of the fabled mountains, disaster struck. One of the

AN ALLIGATOR'S NEST, *1852–53*

LUXURIANT FOREST ON
THE BANK OF THE AMAZON, *1852–53*

National Gallery of Art, Paul Mellon Collection

George Catlin's Recipe for Mosquito Soup

RECIPE — Descending the Missouri or Arkansas rivers in North America, or the Coron-tyns of Uruguay in South America, run your canoe ashore in a thick bottom, just at sundown, having filled your tin kettle about half full of river water, which is very pure and wholesome. Before landing, however, throw a couple of spoonfuls of salt (or, what is better, if you have it, half a pound of salt pork) and one of black pepper into your kettle, and a dozen or so of the small prairie onions (cop-o-blos), a sort of wild onion about the size of a rifle-bullet, and which no travellers in those regions should fail to gather and carry along, as important aids in cooking. In fact, a wild turkey or goose cannot be well roasted without them, as your *stuffing* otherwise will be a complete failure.

"All these things be sure to arrange before you land, as it might be difficult to arrange them on shore. Also, before being put on shore, if you be the cook, you should draw a pair of Indian buckskin leggings over your pantaloons, tying them very tight around the ankles. Leave your hat or cap behind, covering the head with a large silk handkerchief or shawl, passing under the chin, and covering the face as high as the bridge of the nose, and tie it firmly in the back of the neck: then, with a bunch of willow boughs in your left hand to protect your eyes (keeping it constantly in motion), whilst your right hand is free to work with, a thick pair of buckskin gloves or mittens on your hands, and your pantaloons' pockets turned inside out, your person is tolerably secure from all approach, and you may venture to step ashore; but keeping your body and limbs constantly more or less in motion, which will defeat the aim of such probosces as may occasionally have found their way through the imperfect seams or otherwise vulnerable parts of your dress.

"In these heavy wooded bottoms there is always a plenty of dried mulberry limbs and trees, which gather as quick as possible; they burn free, with a light flame and little or no smoke to frighten the mosquitos away. Set your kettle exactly in the middle of the fire, so that the flame will rise equally all around it, and some twelve or fourteen inches above its rim, which is abundantly high.

"The rest of the party, having left you ashore, should then lose no time in paddling into the stream, each one with a bunch of willow-boughs whipping ashore all the insects that are attempting to follow the canoe, and leaving you, the cook, alone to 'walk the kettle,' as one alone concentrates the flying cloud better than several.

"The cloud beginning to gather in promising quantities around you, you may commence walking at a regular pace, with short steps, around the fire and boiling kettle; the swarm will follow in your wake, and, to shorten the distance, they will constantly be flying over the fire, when, their wings being singed, they fall into the kettle; and whilst keeping your eyes clear with the willow-boughs in your left hand, if you aim your blows right, a great many may be thus knocked into the kettle that perhaps are too wary to get their wings burned.

"There is no limited time for this operation, nor any end to the arriving multitudes; but you must be guided entirely by the apparent quantity, by lifting off the kettle occasionally, when the boiling ceases, and their carcasses rise in a large clotted mass on the surface, which with a large wooden spoon you should throw off, as the *fat* is all extracted from them, and their bodies should give way to a fresh supply, in order to obtain the requisite richness of the soup.

"The boiling operation being finished, and the canoe called ashore, the kettle should be handled as quickly as possible, and taken on board; all hands, as they are armed each with a bunch of willow-boughs, will be able to whip the following swarms ashore as the canoe enters the current, over which they never venture to fly more than a few rods.

"Then, landing on some barren sand-bar which has no vegetation, and consequently is uninhabited by these torments, a comfortable night's rest may be enjoyed; and the soup, when it is sufficiently cooled, and the again collected mass of their light and emptied carcasses floating on the surface are again skimmed off with the spoon, and some hard biscuits crumbed in, your kettle of 'Mosquito Soup' is ready for use."

GEO. CATLIN,
Rio Uruguay

mules "stepped its foot into our 'tin pan,' our only gold-washer, and completely broke its bottom through." Now any flecks of gold they might find in the streams were lost to them, for they had no way to "pan" them. Now it was nuggets or nothing.

On and on they went, through the seemingly endless and deserted mountain range, exploring the vertical cliffs for nuggets. At last Catlin spotted a gleaming cluster of them, imbedded in a huge block of quartz. Ever helpful, Caesar fell to with the sledge hammer, sure that the rock held a fortune inside it. But he lost his grip on the handle, and the hammer went flying into the rapids of a stream far below. The frantic search for it failed, and now, entirely lacking in the tools of the miner's trade, they had no choice but to head back to their Amazon headquarters, "actually richer in gold than when we started, by *just two ounces!"*

But Catlin's disappointment was short lived. There *was* treasure for him in South America, though not made of precious metal. The vigorous, outdoor life he had been leading had made Catlin strong again. Here in the jungle, thousands of miles away from his old problems, he was feeling like a young man. And here, even more mysterious than any he had met, lived hundreds and hundreds of Indian tribes. From time to time on his hunt for gold, the artist had glimpsed them, shyly watching from the forest. They could be the source of a whole new Indian Collection! He would travel up the mighty Amazon in a steamboat, sketching and painting, just as he had done on the Missouri River. With stout Caesar's help, he would start all over again.

The Amazon looked peaceful as they headed upsteam. But soon Catlin discovered that it was swarming with life. In the tops of the jacaranda trees huge butterflies hovered. A little lower, the spider monkeys swung from branch to branch, ignoring the somnolent sloths. Parrots, hummingbirds and toucans of every imaginable color and size buzzed and screamed and called from the jungle. At the water's edge giant turtles dozed, and heavy-breathing caymans waited for their prey.

Catlin seldom penetrated the thick forest that lined the banks; he didn't have to. Wherever it went, the steamer *Marajó* drew every Indian within miles running towards the river.

Day after day they chugged ahead, taking on or letting off passengers, crops, livestock, trade goods, fuel, and food. At every stop, Catlin went down the gangplank in search of Indians to paint. But for some reason his old luck was not with him. He went to the Catholic missions in hopes that the *padres* would smooth the way. But his deafness and ignorance of the language made communication almost impossible. Besides, he couldn't explain himself or tell his real name.

After more than a thousand miles, the *Marajó* turned around for the return trip to the Atlantic. But Catlin decided to avoid steamships, with their attention-getting noise and hurried schedule. Instead, he hired a Portuguese trader to steer him quietly and without fanfare down the Amazon, in his little wooden boat. They would drift along, stopping whenever they wished, and for a thousand miles they would search the river for scenes of Indian life for a painter's brush.

Soon Catlin discovered why the Amazon Indians were so wary. In North America, he had found, many Indians feared his "magic": they thought that if Catlin painted their faces, they might somehow lose their souls at the same time. Catlin had always found some way to get around this problem, but here on the Amazon, the Indians had good reason to be "superstitious."

At about this time the scientific world of Europe and America was seized with a sort of "jungle fever." All the great universities were sending droves of scientists to South America. Botanists were there collecting exotic plants in the rain forests. Entomologists from Berlin and Amsterdam were running through the groves with butterfly nets. Zoologists and ornithologists were

Royal Ontario Museum, Toronto

CHASING THE
WILD HORSE, *1857*

On the pampas, or plains of South America, the Indians brought down wild horses and big game by whirling a three-ended rope through the air. At each end of the rope, a heavy stone was tied. It was a lethal weapon, and once it made contact with its victim, it couldn't fail.

trapping bizarre birds and animals and sending the skins home to be stuffed in museums. The Indians had observed all this with wonder and suspicion. Would they be next on the collectors' list?

Not long after he started downstream, Catlin's luck changed. Among the Connibos, he was able to finish some good portraits, and he was overjoyed to have made a real start on his new project at last. But when the pictures were shown to the rest of the tribe, Catlin's old adversary, the medicine man, put in his appearance.

He told his people:

You will never be happy afterwards, if you allow these things [the portraits] to be always awake in the night. My friends, this is only a cunning way this man has to get your skins; and the next thing, they will have glass eyes, and be placed among the skins of the wild beasts and birds and snakes. Don't hurt this man—that is my advice; but he is a bug-catcher and a monkey-skinner.

Catlin was stumped. He had no way of knowing whether these were friendly Indians or cannibals. So he improvised.

"There are your portraits," he said.

I am very sorry that you don't let me have them to show to my friends amongst the white people; but you have resolved to have them destroyed. There are three ways—you may burn them! Or you may drown them! Or you can shoot them! You can destroy them in your own way. Your *medicine man,* who has frightened you about them can tell you, most likely, which way will be the *least dangerous!*

The artist sat back and waited while the Indians discussed this among themselves. Finally they admitted that they were a little afraid of all three. Years later, Catlin recounted the end of the story:

I then said there was another way I had, that of *unpainting* them, from which there could be no possible harm, but it required each one to sit a few minutes for the operation. This seemed to afford them a great relief, and in a few minutes they were all unpainted, covered with a thick coat of clay, which would perfectly preserve them until I wanted to see them again. All were satisfied.

All along the way, Catlin met resistance of one kind or another. Finally he realized that if he were to get any paintings at all, he would have to do it without the Indians' knowing it. So he stayed out of sight under the little canopy that shaded the deck. They would anchor near a village, and while Caesar, dressed in a brilliant red shirt, distracted their attention by firing "Sam," Catlin's revolving rifle, into the sky, the artist got on with his work. If the Indians tired of the fireworks before the great White Medicine Man was finished, the Portuguese trader would get out his fiddle and the Indians would dance away the hours on the sandy beach.

Catlin was never able to really *know* the Indians of South America as he had on the Missouri. They never told their names —nobody on the Amazon ever seemed to give out this information—and he had only a vague idea of their languages, customs or origins. But he did see and paint no less than thirty different tribes in the sixty-nine days he spent going down the Amazon. And in addition to the faces and pastimes of the Indians, he made sketches of wildlife in tributaries and lagoons where no steamship could take him, revelling in "the unknown grandeur of those solitudes—the gloomy but decorated abodes of reptiles and alligators."

There were plenty of hardships along the way. There were poisonous snakes aplenty, and once a huge, over-friendly monkey bit the end of the artist's finger off. But snakes and alligators and jaguars and peccaries were nothing compared to the mosquitoes. From sunup to long after sundown, they made life miserable for Catlin, though for some reason, the Indians were not bothered.

Nevertheless, South America's many mysteries fascinated him. He returned to Europe once or twice but until 1859 he spent most of his time, with Caesar, crisscrossing the unknown conti-

Private collection, Paul Mellon

SHOOTING CONDORS, EASTERN SIERRA OF THE ANDES
1855–56

Adventure followed Catlin up from the steaming Amazon to the high Andes. But, like many of his paintings, this one is a mystery. What has happened to knock Catlin over on his back? And how does the story end? Much as he loved telling stories, he never wrote this one down!

nent, exploring the pampas of Argentina and Uruguay, and climbing into the high Andes on horseback. He even ventured to the southernmost tip of South America, Tierra del Fuego. He tried everything: throwing the *bolas* to bring down wild horses; plunging into the hurly-burly of the "wild ostrich" hunt (though the average rhea was a foot taller than he, and extremely fast on its feet). He learned to love the taste of turtle eggs and alligator meat.

He even fell in love, for a time, with a little Uruguayan girl named Til-tee. Til-tee, "the firefly," was part Portuguese and part Auca Indian. During the brief time he knew her, Catlin was captivated by her beauty and charm. He bought ornaments for her to wear, and when he returned from his first flamingo hunt, he gave her the finest feathers he could find.

But he and Caesar kept on moving. At sixty-one, Catlin steamed through the Straits of Magellan to San Francisco. Catlin found it a discouraging place: "They are all for gold there," he said, "and I am *shy of gold,* having just recovered from it." As soon as they could leave, they did, taking a sailing schooner up to the Northwest coast. On Vancouver Island, the huge Negro had his day, exhibiting Catlin's paintings to the excited Indians. "Caesar kept all comers, and of all languages, amused with the portraits, which he was lecturing on alternately in English, in Spanish, and Lingua Geral [the makeshift language of the Amazon], from which they learned just as much as they would have learned from the squalling of a paroquet or cockatoo."

They put in on the coast of British Columbia, and sailed into Russian waters off Alaska and the Aleutians, and even touched on the Russian mainland. En route, Catlin made portraits of Flatheads, Aleuts, and other Northwest tribes. On the return trip, Catlin and Caesar made an overland trek from the mouth of the Columbia River to the Rockies. On this journey, the artist discovered that he had come a full circle:

The eighth day opened to our view one of the most verdant and beautiful valleys in the world; and on the tenth a distant smoke was observed, and under it the skin-tents, which I at once recognized as of a Crow village. I was again amongst my old friends, the Crows! It was a pleasure that I cannot describe to find myself again amongst mankind as Nature made them, the Crows, whom I had long since thought I had seen for the last time.

And, wonder of wonders, here were Very Sweet Man and the Jumper, whom Catlin had painted at Fort Union twenty years earlier. After a joyous reunion, Caesar and Catlin pushed on, taking a more arduous route this time, for Catlin hated to travel the same way twice. On the way to the Pacific, they met a tired group of New England emigrants heading for Oregon. For a time they rode with the little ox-train, sharing what little food could be found. All along the well-traveled trail, they saw the litter of the great migration: abandoned wagons, broken wheels, and the skeletons of horses and oxen which had fallen, exhausted, in their tracks. They met very few Indians, for they had retreated to safer ground.

By dugout canoe, they then went down the Rio Grande to Matamoros, and by sailing vessel they followed the Mexican coast to the Yucatan peninsula, where remnants of the great, vanished race of Mayan city-builders still raised their little patches of maize. As long as he could be out in the weather, with a challenge in front of him, and nobody in back of him, the self-taught artist from Pennsylvania was content.

But now it was time for the parting of the ways. Caesar Bolla had carried Catlin's portfolio and the Minié rifle for more than ten thousand miles, lightening the artist's burden in more ways than one. At Sisal, on the Yucatan coast, they said goodby; George Catlin headed for Baron von Humboldt and Europe, and Caesar went South, where his old sweetheart waited for him in Belém.

A TROPICAL
FOREST SCENE,
BRAZIL, AROUND *1855*

Deep in the Amazon jungle, two boys fish for their supper with bow and arrow.

Private collection,
photograph courtesy M. Knoedler & Co., Inc., New York

The Tower Room

MORE THAN SIX YEARS HAD PASSED SINCE Catlin dropped out of sight to hunt for gold. He had completely lost touch with his family. They had given him up for lost—or dead. Only one man was getting news from the artist as he traversed the South American continent: his old friend in Berlin, Baron von Humboldt. They wrote to each other about Indian origins, ocean currents, volcanoes and minerals, the aged scientist suggesting topics for Catlin to investigate, and the artist furnishing the answers.

In 1856, while Catlin was in Uruguay, a letter had arrived in Humboldt's crabbed handwriting that was in a different vein.

212

THE TOWER ROOM

My dear friend—

An immense *scrap-book* on the North American Indians, written by Schoolcraft, for the government of the United States, in three huge volumes, has been sent to me as a present; and I find, in looking into it, that he denies the truth of your description of the *"Madan Religious Ceremonies,"* distinctly saying that they are contrary to facts, and that they are the works of your imagination, &c.

Now, my dear esteemed friend, this charge, made by such a man as Schoolcraft, and *"under the authority of the government of the United States,"* to stand in the libraries of the scientific institutions of the whole civilized world, to which they are being sent as presents from your government, is calculated, not only to injure your hard-earned good name, but to destroy the value of your precious works, through all ages, unless you take immediate steps with the government of your country to counteract its effects.

So Henry Schoolcraft had had his revenge. A moment's rudeness long ago would cost Catliṅ his reputation for truthfulness. Unless, that is, the artist could find some way of proving Schoolcraft wrong.

Now, his traveling done, Catlin headed for Brussels, where he barricaded himself in a cheap tenement. There he began a campaign to redeem his reputation that would take the rest of his life. He fired off scores of letters to government officials protesting what Schoolcraft had done to him. He finished up his South American sketches and opened a small, poorly-attended show in Brussels.

And, incredibly, he set out to paint his North American Indian Gallery all over again. From the five hundred-odd little line engravings in his best-selling book, he began to copy. On cheap sheets of Bristol board like the ones Caesar had carried for him over the rivers and mountains of South America, he painted his thirty-year-old memories of Indian life.

When the light in his sparsely furnished room grew too dim for painting, he walked out to a neighborhood cafe, where he

213

spent the evenings writing, writing, writing. The noise of the beer drinkers didn't bother him; he couldn't hear a sound, and the light was good.

During this time Catlin received almost no visitors. Now deaf, he wanted it that way. Conversation, even with friends, only confused and irritated him. But he was not completely shut off from the world. He read the newspapers morning and evening, with their grim dispatches of the "War Between the States" and of the bloody Indian uprisings he had predicted so long ago. In his flat he kept a cage of white mice for company, sharing with them his simple meals of bread and milk.

The long evenings of writing bore fruit; by now almost his only friends were children. They accompanied him in his walks around Brussels, and they listened wide-eyed as he told them, in strange, accented speech, his tales of adventure. So he wrote for them now. "These people are like children; and from what I have seen I am quite sure that if you were amongst them you would learn their true character and their feelings much sooner than your parents would. . . . They would take you by the hand as brothers and sisters."

But still there was the problem of Schoolcraft. Somehow Catlin had to get the true story before the public. Few men then alive, except Catlin, had ever seen the four dreadful days of the O-Kee-Pa. After the smallpox epidemic, the forlorn remnants of the tribe had disappeared into Gros Ventre country.

All Catlin had was his certificate signed by Kipp, Crawford and Bogard and his ineradicable memory of the events he had witnessed in the summer of 1832. With great care, he wrote a full account of the secret ceremony. It was detailed enough to satisfy the most meticulous scientist. Catlin's plan was to furnish a copy of his account to every owner of Schoolcraft's book. Surely he deserved to have his side of the story told. But before he could publish it, he had to have money. He offered some of his work to a London publisher, but the publisher told him it was too old-fashioned to print. Meanwhile, the British Museum sent back a book of sketches, saying it was "not antique enough."

Where *did* he fit? Was there no room for a man like himself in this changed world? George Catlin was almost seventy-four. He had lost his wife, his children and his original dream. He had lost, at least temporarily, the battle with Henry Schoolcraft, and he had nearly outlived the proud last days of his beloved Indians. He had never been fairly compensated in any tangible way for his dedicated career. And his greatest achievement still lay, in crates, in the basement of Joseph Harrison's Philadelphia boiler factory. No one had even opened it.

On a dark winter day late in 1871, George Catlin came home. His brother Francis was there on the dock to greet him, and with him were three lovely women—Libby, Victoria and Clara. Their father scarcely knew them after all these years. His "babes" were all grown up. They were strangers now.

And after thirty-two years, America was a stranger to him, too. The wireless telegraph bridged the continent from sea to sea, and Union Pacific trains rumbled across the prairies where the Indians and buffalo once reigned. The unspoiled rivers where Catlin had paddled his canoe were bustling now with commerce. Factories and cities had sprung up everywhere. The buffalo herds were becoming a thing of the past.

As for the Indians, Catlin's grim prophecies were coming true. The United States government was totally committed now to subduing them completely. The big showdowns with Sitting Bull and Crazy Horse were only a short time away.

Nevertheless, Catlin persevered with his cause. Though the scenes in his new collection were as much as forty years out-of-date, he rented a showroom at the Sommerville Gallery in New York and printed a catalogue. He undoubtedly hoped for the huge crowds of 1838 to come again, but they didn't. The nation had gone on to other things. The Indians were done for, anyhow. Nobody was interested.

Almost half a century had passed since Catlin set out on his life's work. But though he was old, and deaf, and forgotten by his country, his name was well remembered by one old friend from the happy days in Albany. This was Joseph Henry, who was now head of the Smithsonian Institution in Washington. Henry had always admired Catlin's achievements, and he knew of his long, bitter struggle for government recognition. His friend George's career must not be allowed to end this way; he had labored too long and accomplished too much. He deserved some little share of glory before he died. So Henry invited the artist to come to Washington. He could hang his paintings in the National Museum, and he could even have a little room of his own high in one of the Smithsonian's red stone towers.

In the summer of his seventy-fifth year, therefore, George Catlin finally had his showing in the government's museum. The paintings he hung there were but copies of copies; ghostly reminders of the richly-painted originals. Yet Henry's generous gesture kept the artist's hope alive; he began to paint again and to converse with the visitors from official Washington who came to pay their respects. Perhaps he knew that they were only being kind—that there was no way now that the government could ransom his masterpieces from the factory basement. But he kept on hoping. In his tower room, he penned his last petition to Congress. It was just as urgent as the petitions before it. If Catlin suspected now that the cause was lost, the petition didn't show it:

In my old age, after I have devoted a long life of hard labor and all that I have possessed in the world for the history of our country, I am suffering intensely in feelings from the fear that the six hundred Indian portraits and other paintings of the first-named Collection . . . may be cast upon the world without the finish and arrangement which they require, and which no one but myself can give them.

It was not much to ask. He wanted no more than the price he had asked in 1846, and the chance to work on his paintings once more.

But the taxpayers' money was earmarked for other things. The Cavalry needed horses and guns now, for waging war on the Indians. And such things were costly. While American boys were dying on the Western battlefields, there would be no money for pictures—particularly pictures like these.

Joseph Henry sent a letter to Congress vouching for his friend. It did help to clear the artist's name from Schoolcraft's slur, but it did not succeed in changing the legislators' minds.

At last, George Catlin understood that he would never live to see the crates unpacked. He would not get another look at his great work, nor see it displayed permanently before the American people. He became gravely ill. The doctor urged him to keep on painting, for it seemed to make him happy. But one day, George packed away his paints and brushes. His family came and took him to Jersey City, where he died two days before Christmas, 1872.

They buried him in Brooklyn beside his dear wife and baby son.

In time, the treasure was re-discovered. Catlin's crates were found in 1874, after Joseph Harrison's death, still sealed in the boiler-factory basement. Over the years sparks from welders' torches had more than once set the building on fire. Smoke and heat had done their worst, followed by tons of water from the firemen's hoses. And for more than thirty years insects and mice had made homes among the buffalo skins.

When they opened the crates, the workmen had to take almost all of the rotted Indian shirts and moccasins and feathered headdresses and tepees and drums out to the factory yard and bury them. And still the stench of water-logged buffalo robes hung over the place for weeks.

Most of the paintings were thickly coated with soot. A young Smithsonian curator came to have a look, and he could hardly believe that this was actually the famous, long-lost Catlin Indian Gallery, so grimy and woebegone had it become. But he took up Catlin's plea: "Let the government have it," he said.

The Harrison family was glad to be rid of the whole mess, and on May 19, 1879 at the Washington railroad station, the U. S. National Museum took delivery of a freight-car full of 445 weatherbeaten Indian paintings and a few battered, unidentified Indian artifacts. They were a gift outright from the Harrison family, the property of the American people at last. Since then, the paintings have been carefully cleaned and restored to their original appearance. Today, they hang in the National Collection of Fine Arts. Somehow, the beaded dress of Mint (See page 84.) and Four Bears' splendid costume (Pages 80 and 81.) survived. These, with a few arrows, spears, shields, drums, and a beaded cradle are now housed in the Smithsonian's Museum of Natural History.

Catlin's second great set of paintings including his South American scenes (the so-called Cartoon Collection) spent nearly a century in storage at the American Museum of Natural History in New York. But now these, too, belong to the American people. They were bought by Mr. Paul Mellon, and through his generosity, 351 of them now belong to the National Gallery of Art, only four blocks from the original Indian paintings of the 1830's.

Thus, eight hundred of George Catlin's paintings, representing a lifetime of work and thousands of miles of travel, are together at last. A hundred years after the artist's death, his dream has come true. The question he so often asked, "What will become of my Gallery?" has been answered.

Further Reading

Catlin, George, *Episodes from Life Among the Indians, and Last Rambles*. Edited by Marvin Ross Norman (University of Oklahoma Press), 1959. Fully illustrated with selections from the artist's later writings.

Catlin, George, *Letters and Notes on the Manners, Customs, and Condition of the North American Indians*. 2 vols. London, 1841. Catlin's great classic, now available in reprint from Ross & Haines, Inc., Minneapolis (1965).

Ewers, John C., *George Catlin, Painter of Indians and the West*. Washington, D. C. (Smithsonian Institution), 1956. Excellent summary of Catlin's North American work, by the leading Catlin scholar and ethnologist.

Haberly, Loyd, *Pursuit of the Horizon, a Life of George Catlin, Painter and Recorder of the American Indian*. New York, 1948.

Halpin, Marjorie, *Catlin's Indian Gallery, the George Catlin Paintings in the United States National Museum*. Washington, D. C. (Smithsonian Institution), 1965. A good, short summary of the artist's life.

McCracken, Harold, *George Catlin and the Old Frontier*. New York, 1959. A beautifully illustrated, full-length biography.

Plate, Robert, *Palette and Tomahawk, the Story of George Catlin*. New York, 1962. Emphasis on adventure.

Roehm, Marjorie Catlin, *The Letters of George Catlin and His Family, a Chronicle of the American West*. Berkeley, 1966. Fascinating reading; hundreds of private family letters, thoughtfully presented.

Index

223

INDEX